HOW TO PLAN
DIFFERENTIATED READING INSTRUCTION

SOLVING PROBLEMS IN THE TEACHING OF LITERACY
Cathy Collins Block, Series Editor

Recent Volumes

Mindful of Words: Spelling and Vocabulary Explorations 4–8
Kathy Ganske

Finding the Right Texts:
What Works for Beginning and Struggling Readers
Edited by Elfrieda H. Hiebert and Misty Sailors

Fostering Comprehension in English Classes: Beyond the Basics
Raymond Philippot and Michael F. Graves

Language and Literacy Development:
What Educators Need to Know
James P. Byrnes and Barbara A. Wasik

Independent Reading: Practical Strategies for Grades K–3
Denise N. Morgan, Maryann Mraz, Nancy D. Padak, and Timothy Rasinski

Assessment for Reading Instruction, Second Edition
Michael C. McKenna and Katherine A. Dougherty Stahl

Literacy Growth for Every Child:
Differentiated Small-Group Instruction K–6
Diane Lapp, Douglas Fisher, and Thomas DeVere Wolsey

Explaining Reading, Second Edition:
A Resource for Teaching Concepts, Skills, and Strategies
Gerald G. Duffy

Learning to Write with Purpose: Effective Instruction in Grades 4–8
*Karen Kuelthau Allan, Mary C. McMackin,
Erika Thulin Dawes, and Stephanie A. Spadorcia*

Exemplary Literacy Teachers, Second Edition:
What Schools Can Do to Promote Success for All Students
Cathy Collins Block and John N. Mangieri

Literacy Development with English Learners:
Research-Based Instruction in Grades K–6
Edited by Lori Helman

How to Plan Differentiated Reading Instruction:
Resources for Grades K–3
Sharon Walpole and Michael C. McKenna

Reading More, Reading Better
Edited by Elfrieda H. Hiebert

HOW TO PLAN DIFFERENTIATED READING INSTRUCTION

Resources for Grades K–3

Sharon Walpole
Michael C. McKenna

THE GUILFORD PRESS
New York   London

Library of Congress Cataloging-in-Publication Data
Walpole, Sharon.
   How to plan differentiated reading instruction : resources for grades K–3 / by Sharon
Walpole, Michael C. McKenna.
      p. cm.—(Solving problems in the teaching of literacy)
   Includes bibliographical references and index.
   ISBN 978-1-60623-264-4 (pbk.)
   1. Reading (Primary)   2. Individualized instruction.   I. McKenna, Michael C.   II. Title.
LB1525.W175 2009
372.41′7—dc22
                                                                                2008047685

To our students and colleagues
at the University of Virginia and the University of Delaware,
who support our work every time they challenge our thinking

ABOUT THE AUTHORS

Sharon Walpole, PhD, is Associate Professor in the School of Education at the University of Delaware. Her research interests include the design and effects of schoolwide reforms, particularly those involving literacy coaches. Dr. Walpole is coauthor of three previous books with Michael C. McKenna, as well as numerous journal articles. She is the recipient of an Early Career Award from the National Reading Conference for her significant contributions to literacy research and education.

Michael C. McKenna, PhD, is Thomas G. Jewell Professor of Reading at the University of Virginia. His research interests include comprehension in content settings, reading attitudes, technology applications, and beginning reading. Dr. McKenna has published 15 books and more than 100 articles, chapters, and technical reports. His coedited volume *Handbook of Literacy and Technology* received the Edward Fry Book Award from the National Reading Conference and was named an Outstanding Academic Book by *Choice*.

PREFACE

This book, our fourth, represents more than our own ongoing collaboration. It represents our work over time with teachers, literacy coaches, and administrators designing and providing meaningful learning opportunities for children. We are mindful that our university positions are much less demanding than the daily work of these front-line educators. We know this because we watch them. We see the very real demands that life in the classroom places on them. For that reason, we have attempted to put ourselves in their shoes. We have planned lessons, informed by good science and by good sense, in order to reveal processes that can target time and talk and texts. We hope that our lessons will allow teachers to experiment with reasonable and repetitive lesson-planning formats and that they will decide to make these formats their own.

We argue for a definition of differentiated instruction that rests on ongoing informal assessment data and is reasonable to implement. We begin with the basics of our model of differentiated reading instruction, assuming four broad profiles of students. We then invite teachers to try it. We think it is easier to learn the theoretical and design principles that inform this instruction by actually experiencing it. We provide detailed, ready-to-use lesson plans and materials to help teachers hit the ground running. For children whose achievement data reveal needs in phonemic awareness and word recognition, dozens of reproducibles are provided. For fluency, vocabulary, and comprehension, lessons are based on popular, inexpensive trade books. Offering step-by-step guidance to simplify planning and decision making, this book can be used on its own or as a complement to *Differentiated Reading Instruction: Strategies for the Primary Grades*. In fact, this book was born out of our conversations with the many teachers who read and used *Differentiated Reading Instruction* with us.

How to Plan Differentiated Reading Instruction consists of seven chapters. The first provides an overview of our approach and explains how it differs from other differentiation models. The second chapter, linking assessment and instructional planning, describes how our model addresses the emerging demand for increasingly more targeted instruction, called response to intervention. We hope that teachers will see that they really can view their instructional choices for small groups as interventions, and that they can use assessments to plan a sequence of lessons and then gather data to inform their next set of plans.

Chapters 3–6 are the core of the book. They assume that teachers have established a classroom routine in which they read aloud from a rich set of children's books and provide grade-level reading and writing instruction. They also assume that these opportunities alone cannot meet the needs of all students; in fact, they assume that *all* children deserve a portion of their instructional day targeted by a teacher who is addressing their personal instructional needs. We know that this is easier said than done. We try to make our approach reasonable for teachers by drawing lessons from the literature on literacy development. A separate chapter is devoted to each of the four profiles for differentiated instruction that we have defined: (1) phonological awareness instruction and word recognition, (2) word recognition and fluency, (3) fluency and comprehension, and (4) vocabulary and comprehension. These profiles have allowed us to organize instruction that truly meets the children's needs and that takes seriously the reality that teachers have limited time in which to plan and provide such instruction.

A highlight of the book is that each of these chapters also contains multiple sets of 3-week, small-group lesson plans. We wrote the plans in 3-week chunks so that they could dovetail with 6-, 9-, and 12-week calendars for reporting to parents. These plans are ready to use; our students and collaborators are already using them. We are confident that by actually trying a set of the lessons with a group of their children, teachers will be able to understand, fairly quickly, what our approach actually is and whether it will work for them and their children. If the match is right, student success will result in teacher motivation and the book's detailed guide to planning additional lessons will serve as an excellent resource.

When individual teachers gain confidence in the approach on the basis of their own experiences with it, the next step is to build a coordinated effort across the primary grades. Schools with a consistent and reflective commitment to serving the needs of children are exciting places to do the hard work of teaching. The final chapter contains suggestions for making differentiated reading instruction a schoolwide priority. In it, readers will find practical suggestions for scheduling, for collaborative planning, and for conducting formative observations that can allow educators to design a school experience that makes sense for children. We view our model as successful in classrooms and then in schools where it is adapted rather than adopted.

CONTENTS

Chapter 1. **What Do We Mean by Differentiated Reading Instruction?**   1

     MAJOR APPROACHES TO DIFFERENTIATION   2
        Differentiation by Instructional Level   2
        Differentiation by Fluency Level   3
        Differentiation by Assessed Needs   4
     DIFFERENTIATION WITHIN A COMPREHENSIVE
        READING PROGRAM   4
        Instructional Tiers   4
        Instructional Schedules   7
     FOUR POTENTIAL GROUPS   8
     TARGETED, TEMPORARY INSTRUCTION   8
     A PROFESSIONAL CHALLENGE   9
     SUMMARY   10

Chapter 2. **Using Assessments to Plan Differentiated Reading Instruction**   11

     TYPES OF ASSESSMENTS   11
     SYSTEMATIC ASSESSMENT OF NEEDS   13
     USING ASSESSMENTS TO FORM SMALL GROUPS   14
     USING ASSESSMENTS TO PLAN AND EVALUATE INSTRUCTION   15
     USING ASSESSMENTS TO MATCH BOOKS AND CHILDREN   16
        Assessing the Suitability of Books for Fluency Instruction   17
        Assessing the Suitability of Books for Read-Alouds   17
        Assessing the Suitability of Books for Reading   18
     SUMMARY   18

Chapter 3. **Targeting Phonological Awareness and Word Recognition**   19

     WHO NEEDS THIS INSTRUCTION?   19
     WHAT DOES THIS INSTRUCTION LOOK LIKE?   21
     HOW CAN YOU PLAN THIS INSTRUCTION?   22
        Planning for the Basic Alphabet Knowledge Group   23
        Planning for the Using Letter Sounds Group   24
        Planning for the Using Letter Patterns Group   25

STRATEGIES FOR EVERY PUPIL RESPONSE   26
TAKING STOCK   26
SUMMARY   27
APPENDIX 3.1. Lesson Plans   28

Chapter 4. **Targeting Word Recognition and Fluency**   **55**
WHO NEEDS THIS INSTRUCTION?   55
WHAT DOES THIS INSTRUCTION LOOK LIKE?   57
HOW CAN YOU PLAN THIS INSTRUCTION?   61
STRATEGIES FOR EVERY PUPIL RESPONSE   64
TAKING STOCK   65
SUMMARY   67
APPENDIX 4.1. Lesson Plans   68

Chapter 5. **Targeting Fluency and Comprehension**   **96**
WHO NEEDS THIS INSTRUCTION?   96
WHAT DOES THIS INSTRUCTION LOOK LIKE?   97
HOW CAN YOU PLAN THIS INSTRUCTION?   99
   Which Books Should We Choose?   100
   Which Instructional Methods Should We Use?   101
      Syllable Types   103
      Echo Reading   103
      Choral Reading   104
      Partner Reading   105
      Whisper Reading   106
   Which Questions Should We Ask?   107
STRATEGIES FOR EVERY PUPIL RESPONSE   108
TAKING STOCK   108
SUMMARY   110
APPENDIX 5.1. Lesson Plans   111

Chapter 6. **Targeting Vocabulary and Comprehension**   **118**
WHO NEEDS THIS INSTRUCTION?   119
WHAT DOES THIS INSTRUCTION LOOK LIKE?   120
HOW CAN YOU PLAN THIS INSTRUCTION?   121
   Which Words and Strategies Should We Teach?   122
   Which Instructional Methods Should We Use?   124
STRATEGIES FOR EVERY PUPIL RESPONSE   129
   How Can We Design a Lesson?   130
TAKING STOCK   131
SUMMARY   132
APPENDIX 6.1. Lesson Plans   133

Chapter 7. **Making Differentiation Schoolwide**   **159**
FACTORS INFLUENCING MOTIVATION   160
USABLE STUDENT ACHIEVEMENT DATA   161
   Implications for Teachers   161
   Implications for Teacher Leaders   162
   Mistakes to Avoid   162
FLEXIBLE DECISION MAKING   162
   Implications for Teachers   163
   Implications for Teacher Leaders   163
   Mistakes to Avoid   164

STRATEGIES FOR REFLECTION 165
   Implications for Teachers 165
   Implications for Teacher Leaders 166
   Mistakes to Avoid 166
PROBLEM-SOLVING CLIMATE 167
   Implications for Teachers 167
   Implications for Teacher Leaders 167
   Mistakes to Avoid 168
A FINAL PLEA 168

References 169

Index 173

Chapter 1

WHAT DO WE MEAN BY DIFFERENTIATED READING INSTRUCTION?

For those of us who work to serve an increasingly diverse population of children in elementary schools, research and policy have created a perfect storm. Federal mandates for assessment and disaggregation of data identify groups of children who need more attention. Researchers design and test instructional strategies to target the needs of specific readers. Districts invest in instructional materials and in professional development in efforts to differentiate their curriculum so that more and more children can attain meaningful levels of achievement. At best, these efforts may be overwhelming. At worst, they may yield an incoherent instructional patchwork. In fact, teachers may be suffering from an embarrassment of riches as they try to navigate their choices.

We have always been attracted to the logical principle named for the 14th-century logician William of Ockham. Ockham's razor is a maxim that we can apply to the choices teachers face as they try to meet the needs of all of their students: All other things being equal, the simplest solution is the best. In *Differentiated Reading Instruction: Strategies for the Primary Grades* (Walpole & McKenna, 2007), we identified simple instructional strategies with strong research pedigrees—strategies that could be used to target small-group instruction in a skills-based instructional model. Since that time, we have had the great privilege to learn with and from principals, literacy coaches, and teachers who have read the book and used it to change some aspects of their instruction. What we have found is that some aspects of our model were transparent, and other aspects were not. Many teachers who read that book were able to incorporate new instructional strategies; many teachers appreciated the scripts we provided to make those strategies more efficient. But many teachers whom we have visited were still struggling to make their planning more effective and more efficient. They could understand how to plan one lesson, but admitted to having problems planning a series of gradually more complex lessons. We turned this problem into an opportunity and again sought the simplest solution.

This is not a book about instructional strategies. It is a book about instructional planning. We wrote it by identifying predictable bottlenecks in reading development, and by writing a series of brief, targeted, measurable lesson plans to address those challenges. Then we unpacked our own thinking, trying to make explicit those choices that we made as we planned. In the chapters that follow, we provide both those sets of plans and our instructional decisions. The simplest solution to deep understanding of this instruction is to actually try it (using the plans we have designed) and, if it works, use our narrative and our models to understand and replicate the planning process.

Before a teacher makes that commitment, though, we present the assumptions that we make about when and why differentiated reading instruction is important. We do that by briefly taking stock of historical trends and the contributions of our colleagues to our current thinking. Then we nest our model within the broader confines of reading instruction, and challenge teachers to set the stage for differentiation before jumping in. Finally, we introduce the "simplest solution" we can envision: four different predictable profiles of reading development where differentiation might be necessary.

MAJOR APPROACHES TO DIFFERENTIATION

Differentiation by Instructional Level

The traditional approach to differentiated instruction began with estimating the child's instructional reading level. To do so, the teacher administered an informal reading inventory (IRI) consisting of a series of graded passages followed by comprehension questions. The idea was to advance through the passages until the child began to experience frustration. Criteria for word recognition accuracy and comprehension were applied to determine the highest level at which the child was likely to succeed. This level was then used to select reading materials. The passage levels that make up most commercial IRIs are the same as the conventional levels of a basal reading series. This alignment made placement easy. If the IRI estimate of the child's instructional reading level was primer, then the child would be placed in the primer level of the basal reading series. An elementary teacher would have had several levels of the basal reading series available in the classroom. Students were assigned to levels based on their instructional reading levels, so that several groups, each at a different reading level, would receive instruction in the corresponding basal reader throughout the literacy block.

There were many problems with this approach to differentiated reading instruction. A major difficulty was that the IRI estimates of the instructional level were not particularly reliable (Spector, 2005). In fact, IRIs have always suffered from a host of measurement problems that make it impossible for them to be more than crude indicators of a child's proficiency (see McKenna & Stahl, 2009). Another problem was that once a child was placed at a particular basal level, the introduction of skills in a variety of strands (e.g., phonics, sight words, vocabulary, etc.) is the same for all children at that level. Individual differences in their skill needs were ignored, and all children received the same instruction in all of the strands. Finally, once a child was placed within a basal level, the placement was all but permanent (Barr, 1992). This was because teachers were reluctant to move a child to the next level, even when his or her proficiency seemed to warrant such a move. Leapfrogging a level would have meant that a great deal of skill instruction would have been skipped. This all-but-permanent group placement did not prove especially effective and led in many cases to disparaging group identity (Eagles, Robins, and Vultures), with evidence that placement in a low group led to negative attitudes toward reading (Wallbrown, Brown, & Engin, 1978).

Although a case can be made for estimating the instructional reading level as part of a basal reading series, basal readers are no longer used in this way. In the early 1990s, basal authors began to recommend that all children receive grade-level instruction. That is, they all read the same reading selections, some receiving more support than others. Differentiation occurs at a different time during the literacy block and materials such as leveled readers are provided for this purpose.

Differentiation by Fluency Level

The many problems with the practice of differentiating by instructional reading level led to a widely used alternative championed by Irene Fountas and Gay Su Pinnell (1996). Their alternative is to differentiate by estimating a child's fluency level and planning small-group instruction around short trade books that have been carefully leveled. These leveled books have far more gradations than a conventional basal reading series. Moreover, care is taken to ensure that levels are sequenced as accurately as possible. This is accomplished by considering a variety of factors in addition to readability, such as print layout, illustrations, and patterned language. Children are grouped by level, and then differentiated instruction requires multiple copies of books at that level. These levels are drawn from a leveled book library. The teacher guides the children as they read the book aloud, starting with a picture walk and eliciting thoughtful interactions with the children throughout, including predictions and questions. As the year proceeds, the group moves from one level of text to the next. The principal rationale for the guided reading approach is that oral reading practice of an appropriate text, accompanied by comprehension instruction, is the key to fostering proficiency.

We readily acknowledge that guided reading has helped innumerable children attain proficiency, and the approach remains highly popular across the United States. At the same time, however, we believe that it is not the best approach for all children. For youngsters who have acquired a full range of word recognition skills—and are therefore in a position to increase their speed and accuracy through practice—guided reading is perhaps an ideal approach. For children who are not yet proficient decoders, we argue that small-group time can be better used in other ways. We support Chall's (1983/1996) idea that a child must pass through discernable stages en route to proficiency. Fluency is one of those stages, but it is not the first. An emphasis on fluency during small-group instruction assumes that the child has progressed to the point where such instruction is likely to be effective.

Differentiation by Assessed Needs

For children at the fluency stage, our approach to differentiated instruction looks very much like guided reading. However, for children who have not reached this stage, or have progressed beyond it, our approach looks very different. Differentiated instruction is best planned on the basis of systematic assessment that goes beyond estimating a child's instructional reading level or fluency level. We argue that it is essential to determine needs more specifically so that planning for small-group work can target those needs. Assessment begins with screening tests designed to identify strengths and concerns in several areas. Where concerns arise, diagnostic assessments are given next in order to determine specific needs. Assessments are administered periodically in order to gauge the impact of instruction. We propose a 3-week cycle of assessment and instruction. This cycle requires that a teacher must reconsider the needs of individual children. In doing so, the teacher may conclude that a child's needs are best met within a different group. Consequently, small groups are flexible. They are not permanent. There are no Vultures.

There is compromise involved in this process. For example, struggling readers often present a host of needs, each of which is a potential target of differentiated instruction. However, not all of these needs can be effectively addressed during a lesson that is 15 or 20 minutes long. Consequently, the teacher must choose among the assessed needs and focus on no more than two. Over time, the children in each type of small group will, through targeted temporary instruction, achieve an "upward mobility" toward more advanced groups in which higher-level proficiencies are targeted. The remainder of this book outlines this process in detail and provides extensive models for how it can be implemented.

DIFFERENTIATION WITHIN A COMPREHENSIVE READING PROGRAM

Most districts would argue that they have a comprehensive, coherent, seamless, research-based, assessment-driven approach to reading instruction. However, such rhetoric rarely finds its way through classroom doors in systematic ways. Before anyone tries our differentiation model, this rhetoric must actually be enacted. We try to simplify the process.

Instructional Tiers

We first learned of the concept of tiered instruction through the web-based resources of the Texas Education Agency (see *www.texasreading.org/utcrla/materials/3tier_letter. asp*). The concept resonated with us, connecting to our earliest work with literacy coaches implementing schoolwide reading programs (Walpole & McKenna, 2004). Tiered instruction is meant to be a flexible framework for implementing sound instruction designed to address the assessed needs of children. Tiered instruction is prevention oriented (in that it attempts to head off problems by providing sound initial instruction) and reasonable (in that it assumes that prevention will be imperfect, and some children will need additional instruction). The concept of tiered instruction forms the basis for the federally mandated response-to-intervention (RTI) model. Figure 1.1 provides a visual representation. The size of each tier represents the relative number of children served.

The first tier is core reading instruction. "Core instruction" is a much-maligned term, calling to mind scripted programs that forbid teacher choices and silence teacher voices. That definition is not the only one, however. A core reading program is a set of instructional practices and materials informed by scientifically based reading research. It most often employs a commercial basal reading series, but that is not required. And if a basal is chosen, there is no requirement that it be a scripted one or that teachers forgo all instructional decisions. Rather, a core program, to us, is that set of choices that each grade-level team makes collaboratively about just what grade-level instruction will entail. A core program always includes vocabulary and comprehension instruction, and also includes types and amounts of phonemic awareness instruction, phonics and word recognition instruction, and fluency instruction appropriate to the grade level. A good core program is systematic (meaning that skills are taught and practiced and reviewed in a logical order) both within a grade level and across grade levels. A core program is a road map that directs teachers in the same school to provide children in the same grade with a particular sequence of learning opportunities.

The second characteristic of Tier I instruction is a set of basic assessments. This set must include some type of benchmark testing of all children at least three times each year. That testing is used to monitor the extent to which the core program is meeting the needs of the children in general and to identify children who need additional instruction. The assessments are scheduled in advance and data are summarized systematically.

The final characteristic of Tier I instruction is support for teachers. If schools are to provide children with a high-quality, research-based core program, teachers need ongoing professional support. We have worked with many literacy coaches hired to provide

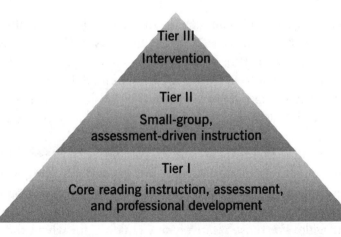

FIGURE 1.1. Tiered instruction.

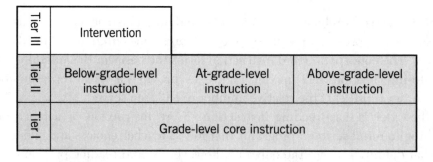

FIGURE 1.2. Our interpretation of tiered instruction.

this support in the form of job-embedded professional development cycles of theory, demonstration, practice, and feedback (Joyce & Showers, 2002). They help teachers collaborate to improve the quality of the core program, and they interpret the assessments that are used to judge its effectiveness. Our differentiation model assumes that *all three* components of Tier I are firmly in place.

Tier II instruction is the focus of our differentiation lessons. Tier II is additional daily small-group instruction, targeted to address students' needs. In many models, only struggling children qualify for this instruction. That is, children identified in the Tier I benchmarking assessments as performing below grade level receive additional instruction right away. We choose to extend this right to all children. Grade-level designations are fairly arbitrary, after all. And in this arbitrary system, struggling children, grade-level children, and even above-grade-level children deserve to have some portion of their school day devoted to their needs. In a given classroom, all groups might not be represented. Some classrooms have no below-grade-level children; others have no children achieving above grade level. This is not important. The important fact is that all children can be served. Because of our commitment to this idea, we have had to make our small-group instruction brief enough that at least three groups can be served during the reading block.

Finally, tiered instruction also anticipates that some children will need very intensive, very specialized instruction. Tier III instruction is typically delivered by other professionals (e.g., reading specialists or special educators) using specially designed curriculum materials. We *do not* consider our differentiation model to be appropriate for Tier III instruction. Our differentiation model, then, is not well represented by a pyramid. It looks more like Figure 1.2, with the shaded areas planned and provided by the classroom teacher for all children.

To sum up, we assume that teachers will first attend to Tier I, specifying the content of core instruction, choosing benchmark assessments, and engaging in systematic professional development. If they have accomplished those three goals, our differentiation model can be used for Tier II, and can extend Tier II opportunities to all children, not just those who struggle. For those relatively few children for whom the combination of high-quality core instruction and daily high-quality differentiated reading instruction are insufficient, Tier III provides a safety net.

Instructional Schedules

Tiered instruction requires instructional schedules. When we think of instructional schedules, we think of much more than the school's schedule for instructional blocks, specials, and lunch. Rather, we think of an exact structure that teachers will use to allocate their most precious resource—time. The simplest solution for the Tier I and Tier II instruction to be provided is through grade-level core instruction for a portion of the reading block and differentiated instruction for another portion of the reading block. A broad-brushstroke model is presented in Figure 1.3.

We assume that, no matter what the make-up of a heterogeneous classroom, children can be divided into three skills-based groups. The teacher first spends half of the instructional block providing grade-level instruction to all children, and then serves each of three different groups for 15 minutes while the others engage in meaningful reading practice. We use the term *reading practice* rather than *centers* or *work stations* because it highlights the goal rather than the place. In fact, we recommend that teachers simplify reading practice and connect it to reading instruction by considering these tasks:

1. Look for materials already in the commercial program that are better suited to practice than to instruction.
2. Consider daily paired oral readings and readings of previously read texts or of additional texts at appropriate levels of difficulty.
3. Consider an activity linked directly to the daily read-aloud. Children can write in response to that text every day.
4. Consider a daily activity linked directly to differentiated instruction. Children can work in pairs to practice the skills and strategies from the last small-group session.

We know that many teachers will say that they cannot complete their grade-level instruction in only 45 minutes. We suggest that they work with colleagues to make sure they are not wasting time during that instruction. Not all activities in a basal reading

Grade-Level Core Reading Instruction 45 minutes		
Group 1 15 minutes	Group 2 15 minutes	Group 3 15 minutes
Differentiated instruction	Reading practice	Reading practice
Reading practice	Differentiated instruction	Reading practice
Reading practice	Reading practice	Differentiated instruction

FIGURE 1.3. A basic plan for grade-level and differentiated instruction.

series are important. In fact, with many series, it would be impossible to use all of the ideas and suggestions for a particular theme even if reading instruction took every minute of the instructional day. Teachers can work together to sort core instructional components from extension and enrichment activities. They can also moderate and control instructional pacing so that early introductions and reviews are fast. We have observed many grade-level lessons in which the instructional pace was simply too slow to maximize student engagement and interaction. Picking up the pace of grade-level instruction may serve both to improve its effectiveness *and* to create time for differentiated reading instruction.

FOUR POTENTIAL GROUPS

If teachers are willing to organize their grade-level instruction and design high-quality reading practice, they are ready to fill in those three differentiated instructional blocks. Again, in our search for the simplest solution, we are committed to only four basic differentiation groups, each group addressing only two aspects of reading development. Figure 1.4 names them.

It is important for teachers to understand that our simple solution—attending to only two things at a time—is also an unbalanced solution. We actually would not want teachers who do not have grade-level core instruction in place to use our model. We represent our model as a staircase to remind teachers that the success of their instruction can be judged by the speed with which children ascend the stairs, ready for more challenging differentiated tasks.

TARGETED, TEMPORARY INSTRUCTION

As we have watched teachers delivering small-group instruction, we have been struck by how often the tasks appear to be too easy for the children. Small groups are costly in terms of planning and management. For that reason, we want the instruction to be as challenging as possible. Reading practice will happen when children are not with the teacher. Reading instruction must be challenging for all. We have come to see that chal-

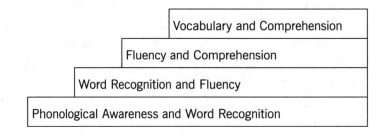

FIGURE 1.4. Four potential differentiation groups.

lenging instruction is characterized by the need for modeling. In fact, you will see in our lessons that teacher modeling is constant, consistent, and explicit.

You will also see a new commitment to every-pupil-response strategies. After teachers model, you will see that they use simple techniques to have every child thinking and responding. We have borrowed some of the techniques from our special education colleagues, and all of them are designed to increase the chances that all children will be attending every minute that they are provided differentiated instruction.

And, finally, our simplest solution involves repetition. This time, though, words and texts are not repeated. Rather, instructional strategies are repeated, so that both teacher and children know exactly what will happen when they gather for their small-group lesson. This saves time because the teacher has to teach the procedures only once. It also allows us to plan new content each day, holding constant the format of the instructional delivery.

A PROFESSIONAL CHALLENGE

We have planned 12 separate cycles of differentiated reading instruction. Most are presented as a sequence of 14 lessons, with one day reserved for assessment. These lessons are designed to use teacher time efficiently and to help children climb the steps that they need to climb to surpass grade-level expectations. Figure 1.5 shows the focus of each of set of lessons, nested within our four areas of focus.

Our professional challenge to teachers is this: Administer and interpret assessments as we recommend in the next chapter. Form one small group and decide where the children are on the staircase. Then read the chapter that deals with that stair step. Choose the set of lessons that most closely addresses the children's needs. And try them out. If

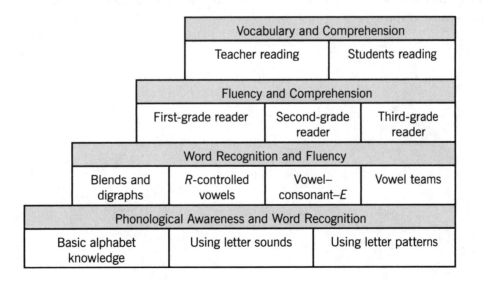

FIGURE 1.5. Differentiated instruction cycles.

they are an improvement on your previous differentiation attempts, reread the chapter to better understand our planning process, and then plan your own lessons. Our hope is that success with any one group will create the motivation to add another group.

We are chasing Ockham's razor. Our first problem was making our model of differentiation more accessible. The simplest solution we could generate was to script initial lessons so that teachers could really experience the model and decide whether it is right for them. Our second problem was to help teachers plan their own lessons. The simplest solution we could generate was to experience the planning ourselves and document our thinking. Differentiation is a complex task. Even the simplest solutions are not really simple. We are hoping, though, that these supports are useful.

SUMMARY

Our model of differentiation is not the same thing as guided reading. It is a more skills-focused model. It assumes a tiered instructional program, with at least some portion of instruction reserved for grade-level work. It assumes that assessments are given and used to make instructional decisions. It assumes that a reading block can be built to address both grade-level instruction and differentiated instruction for all children. It assumes that children with very severe needs will also have access to additional instruction, outside of the reading block.

We predict that there are four potential types of differentiated lessons, each addressing two specific skill areas. Within those four types, we have anticipated a set of likely needs and we have written lessons to address them. Our hope is that these lessons will provide a rich enough entry into the model that teachers will develop momentum. If they have the will, then our planning descriptions may be enough to support a truly differentiated classroom—one in which the teacher understands and targets the needs of students temporarily and directly.

Chapter 2

USING ASSESSMENTS TO PLAN DIFFERENTIATED READING INSTRUCTION

Assessments are important for small-group differentiated instruction for three reasons. First, they permit the teacher to decide which children will benefit most from instruction with a particular focus. Second, they provide guidance in choosing which skills to target in a series of lessons. Finally, they form the basis of determining whether small-group instruction has been effective and deciding which group will best serve each child during the next 3-week cycle. Ultimately, the question of group placement arises at the beginning and end of the cycle, and assessment is best viewed as a recurring process. Figure 2.1 portrays this process.

TYPES OF ASSESSMENTS

We need to be clear about the three types of assessments included in this cycle. A *screening* assessment provides a quick indicator of how well a student is progressing in a fairly broad area, such as decoding or oral reading fluency. A grade-level passage selected from

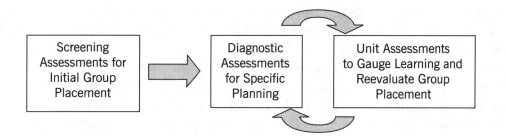

FIGURE 2.1. The assessment cycle for small-group instruction.

the materials a teacher is using can be used to screen oral fluency, for example, with a child's performance being judged against grade norms or benchmarks. This is an example of curriculum-based measurement (see Hosp, Hosp, & Howell, 2007). Standardized screening instruments can also be used for the same purpose, such as those found in the Phonological Awareness Literacy Screening (PALS) and Dynamic Indicators of Basic Early Literacy Skills (DIBELS) batteries. A *diagnostic* assessment breaks down the area targeted into specific skills. It is only given after a screening test has signaled a potential problem. Such an assessment can be informal and might consist of a skills inventory. A *unit* assessment is administered at the end of a 3-week cycle to judge the effectiveness of the small-group instruction the children have received. A unit assessment is always informal and can be teacher constructed. It measures the extent to which instruction has helped children acquire the skills identified by the diagnostic assessment.

Not all of these assessments are relevant to every small group. Word recognition skills are easily assessed using diagnostic measures, and we have useful, easy-to-administer inventories of phonemic awareness, phonics, and sight word knowledge (McKenna & Stahl, 2009). But higher-level skills cannot be addressed in this way. In fact, there are no diagnostic assessments available in the areas of fluency, vocabulary, and comprehension. This might come as a surprise since screening measures are available in all three of these areas.

Fluency problems are addressed not by diagnostic assessments but by administering screening assessments at lower levels. If problems are identified at these underlying levels (phonemic awareness, phonics, or sight word knowledge), then diagnostic assessments are administered in these areas and instruction is planned to address the deficits. If a screening indicates that fluency is a concern *and* underlying problems are ruled out, then fluency is a good target for instruction and a guided reading format is likely to be successful. If, however, underlying problems are identified through lower-level screenings, then they must be addressed before fluency instruction is likely to be successful.

The case of comprehension and vocabulary is different for two reasons. First, there are *no* lower levels. These dimensions of reading gradually develop as the child learns new words and acquires more sophisticated oral language structures. Second, a diagnostic assessment would reveal specific deficits to address through instruction, and there is simply no way of subdividing these areas for this purpose. In the case of vocabulary, a diagnostic test would identify specific words whose meanings are unfamiliar to a child. The sheer number of words makes such a task unrealistic. In the case of comprehension, it is true that attempts have been made to delineate this broad area into a relatively small number of component skills (e.g., inferring sequences, noting details, etc.), but attempts to devise assessments that reliably measure these skills have failed (McKenna & Stahl, 2009; Schell & Hanna, 1981).

All of this is good news for teachers as they use assessments to plan differentiated reading instruction for small groups. Instruction in fluency, vocabulary, and comprehension is not planned on the basis of skills identified through diagnostic assessments. Effective fluency instruction depends on providing systematic practice in appropriate texts. Effective vocabulary instruction involves targeting words that a teacher knows will be useful, even though children's knowledge of these words will be at different levels of sophistication. Effective comprehension instruction relies on revisiting key skills and strategies in new texts, a policy that does not require diagnostic assessment.

SYSTEMATIC ASSESSMENT OF NEEDS

Planning small-group instruction that is well tailored to the needs of individual children requires a systematic approach to gathering information (McKenna & Walpole, 2005). In our experience, there is no better framework for accomplishing systematic assessment than the cognitive model of reading assessment, introduced by Steven Stahl, Kuhn, and Pickle (1999) and revised by McKenna and Katherine Dougherty Stahl (2009). Figure 2.2 shows how problems in comprehending grade-level text can be tracked backward along three dimensions to underlying skill deficits.

The arrows, moving from left to right, signify developmental milestones that are roughly sequential. All arrows lead to our goal—reading comprehension of grade-level texts. For students not achieving that goal, we work backward with screenings to find the source of their problem and then forward with diagnostic assessments to help us address the problem with instruction.

In this system, the fact that a child cannot comprehend grade-level texts leads to three series of questions. The first series of questions involves oral reading, and it is

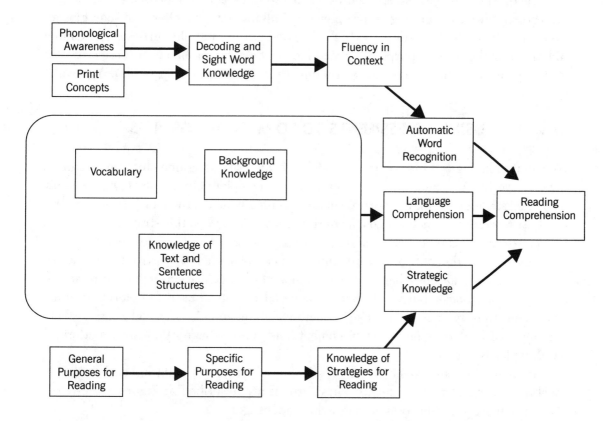

FIGURE 2.2. The revised cognitive model of reading assessment.

represented on the top pathway. If a child's word recognition is automatic, no additional questions are required in this area. If it is not, the teacher must next consider oral fluency in terms of grade-level expectations. If screening assessments (typically grade-level passages read aloud to measure reading rate and accuracy) indicate that the child's performance falls short of these expectations, the teacher moves on to screenings in decoding and sight word vocabulary. A deficit in decoding leads to screening in phonemic awareness and basic print concepts. A skills inventory in phonemic awareness is given if the screening indicates a problem there. Likewise, a skills inventory in phonics and a sight word inventory are given if phonemic awareness is strong but decoding is weak. This logical process leads to a reliable notion of the kind of word recognition instruction that will benefit the child the most.

The second series of questions concerns oral language development. The three components are vocabulary, background knowledge, and knowledge of text and sentence structures. Unlike word recognition, they are not linked in domino fashion. This makes systematic assessment more difficult because all three components need to be addressed. Screening instruments are available for vocabulary. These include individual assessments, group achievement subtests, and core assessments. Background knowledge and knowledge of text and sentence structures are more elusive. A teacher's interaction with a child may offer clues into these components. However, we believe that vocabulary is a reasonable indicator in this area.

The third series of questions focuses on how well the child understands that the way we read will differ depending on our purpose. Talking with the child can soon give an indication of whether an awareness has developed of the multiple purposes for reading and, if not, of the general purpose for reading. We find that problems in these areas are relatively rare, and they do not figure prominently in our planning for small-group work.

USING ASSESSMENTS TO FORM SMALL GROUPS

We can use the logic of the cognitive model to guide us in assigning children to groups. Because we are not concerned with conducting a complete clinical work-up, we apply the model strategically for the purpose of determining which of the four principal groups will best represent the needs of each child. Figure 2.3 displays this strategy in terms of key questions that can be answered on the basis of quick screening assessments.

Note that we do not begin by attempting to estimate a child's instructional reading level. As we indicated in Chapter 1, we consider this information important in selecting appropriate books, but we do not recommend that it be used to determine group placement. More basic screenings (in fluency, decoding, and phonological awareness) are administered to determine group placement, and simple diagnostic tests are administered to plan instruction.

Applying this assessment strategy results in five groups of children, each with reasonably similar instructional needs. These groups are described in Figure 2.4, ordered from most to least advanced in literacy achievement.

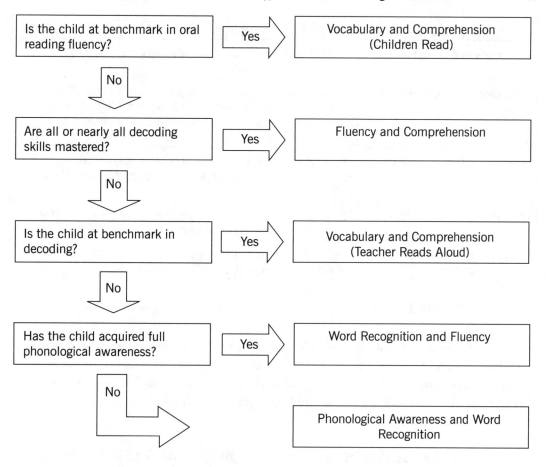

FIGURE 2.3. A decision strategy for forming small groups.

USING ASSESSMENTS TO PLAN AND EVALUATE INSTRUCTION

Children in the lowest two groups—Word Recognition and Fluency and Phonological Awareness and Word Recognition—will require additional assessments in order to plan instruction. Remember that word recognition and phonological awareness can be broken down into component skills and that we can use assessments to determine which of these skills to teach. We can use very similar assessments to gauge the extent to which our 3-week small-group cycle has produced the effects on learning that we intended. Of course, we need to rely on end-of-cycle assessments for the other three groups as well. For fluency, the assessment may involve a grade-level passage read orally. For vocabulary, it may involve a check of the specific words targeted during the 3-week cycle. For comprehension, we do not conduct assessments at the end of a cycle because it is too difficult to measure progress in this area reliably (Stahl, 2009). Instead, we return periodically to fluency screenings to ensure that students continue to demonstrate at least grade-level performance as time passes and as fluency benchmarks increase.

Group	Characteristics of Group Members
Vocabulary and Comprehension (2–3)	These children can read grade-level materials fluently.
Vocabulary and Comprehension (K–1)	Although they have not yet mastered the full range of word recognition skills, children are at benchmark in phonological awareness and decoding and therefore do not need small-group work in these areas.
Fluency and Comprehension	These children have mastered the full range of word recognition skills but need practice in applying these skills automatically.
Word Recognition and Fluency	These children are below benchmark in decoding, but they have acquired strong phonological awareness.
Phonological Awareness and Word Recognition	These children are below benchmark in decoding and have not yet achieved adequate phonological awareness.

FIGURE 2.4. Characteristics of children in each type of small group.

Figure 2.5 suggests the end-of-cycle assessments we recommend to gauge the impact of instruction and to make a decision about which group would be most appropriate for each child in the next cycle. Remember that the 15th lesson in each cycle is reserved for this purpose. No time outside of the small-group session should be required.

USING ASSESSMENTS TO MATCH BOOKS AND CHILDREN

Whenever an activity requires children to read, questions arise about the difficulty of the text. Is it too easy for students to benefit? It is so difficult that they will be

Group	Possible Assessments to Gauge Impact
Vocabulary and Comprehension (2–3)	Vocabulary assessment of targeted words. Fluency assessment if teacher suspects that child may have fallen below benchmark.
Vocabulary and Comprehension (K–1)	Vocabulary assessment of targeted words. Screenings in word recognition if teacher suspects that child may have fallen below benchmark.
Fluency and Comprehension	Fluency screening on grade-level passage.
Word Recognition and Fluency	Fluency screening on grade-level passage. Phonics assessment for taught patterns. Sight word assessment for taught words.
Phonological Awareness and Word Recognition	Informal phonological awareness inventory. Phonics assessment for taught letter names and sounds. Sight word assessment for taught words.

FIGURE 2.5. End-of-cycle assessments for each group.

frustrated? To what extent can the teacher's availability make a more difficult text acceptable? To what extent does the purpose for reading make a difference in the suitability of a text? McKenna and Robinson (2009) suggest that there are two basic ways of judging the suitability of the text: (1) estimating its difficulty level (readability) and comparing that estimate with some independent measure of a student's reading level or (2) judging the match between the student and the text by observing how well the student performs. We recommend that these approaches be combined in a two-step process:

1. Make a preliminary judgment about whether a book is suitable for a group.
2. Try out the book and judge whether it is actually suitable in the lesson format you are using.

Differentiated lessons for three of our groups require the teacher to make these judgments.

Assessing the Suitability of Books for Fluency Instruction

The books children will read in the Fluency and Comprehension group must be comprehensible. This observation may seem obvious, but when the main goal is to foster fluency, it is possible to lose sight of the fact that they must also be easily understood. In Chapter 5, we introduce some web resources to help you make the initial selections, but there are no guarantees. At the end of the first text segment, asking a few literal-level comprehension questions will provide an indicator of the book's suitability. In the rare case that the content and language prove to be beyond the grasp of the group, it will be necessary to try a different book the next day.

Assessing the Suitability of Books for Read-Alouds

Kindergarten and first-grade teachers will conduct read-alouds for the Vocabulary and Comprehension group. These children lack the decoding skills needed to attempt the reading themselves, but because they are making good progress in acquiring these skills small-group instruction centers on vocabulary and comprehension. The read-aloud format means that the books should be at or near the children's *listening level*—the highest level of text that the children can comprehend when it is read aloud to them. We do not recommend attempting to measure listening level directly. There are ways of doing so but they require too much time. A better approach is to begin with books written at a low second-grade level and try them out. The web resources we discuss in Chapter 5 can prove useful in making these choices. However, their actual suitability for a particular group can only be determined after the read-aloud begins. Our lessons on sea mammals at the end of Chapter 6 incorporate frequent pauses to make the experience more interactive. These pauses will produce the information needed to judge whether the book is too difficult. Are the children able to respond and contribute in ways that demonstrate their comprehension? If not, another choice will need to be made.

Assessing the Suitability of Books for Reading

Second- and third-grade teachers will require their fluent readers to read and comprehend books with limited support in small-group lessons. Again, readability estimates can help a teacher make initial, tentative choices, but the true suitability of the match between the group and the book can only be determined by observing children's responses to questions. The first text segment of a new book is critical for making this determination. Although the principal focus is on comprehension strategies and arriving at conclusions that are beyond the literal level of understanding, asking a few questions with explicit answers can provide a quick indicator of whether the book is too hard.

SUMMARY

Assessments are needed to make group assignments, to plan instruction, and to gauge the effectiveness of that instruction at the end of the 3-week cycle. Screening assessments can be useful for assigning children to the group that will benefit them the most, but diagnostic assessments must be used to plan instruction in the areas of phonological awareness and word recognition. Diagnostic assessments are not used in the areas of fluency, vocabulary, or comprehension. Assessing the impact of instruction is informal. It may involve skills inventories, fluency checks, or teacher-constructed tests of the vocabulary introduced.

Coordinating the assessments used to make group assignments is best accomplished through the cognitive model of reading assessment. This model suggests a logical sequence of questions to guide teachers in forming the best groups. Although using this strategy is not an exact process, it leads in most cases to groupings that are most likely to benefit individual children.

Another dimension of assessment involves gauging the match between the children and the books that will be used for fluency development and for comprehension and vocabulary work. A two-step process can guide teachers in making these judgments. The first step is to examine the books in advance, using databases to estimate level of difficulty. The second step is to take stock of children's comprehension during the first lesson with a new book.

We have three assessment targets. We assess children's needs. We assess the difficulty of the texts we choose. And we assess the effects of our instruction. In the remainder of this book, we put these assessment ideas into context as we explore strategies for planning differentiated reading instruction.

Chapter 3

TARGETING PHONOLOGICAL AWARENESS AND WORD RECOGNITION

Our first set of options for differentiated instruction is the most basic pairing—phonological awareness and word recognition. A child who is in this group cannot yet attack even simple unknown words like *cat* or *pig*; this child may be lacking either knowledge of letter sounds, the ability to blend sounds, or the basic alphabetic principle—the concept that the sounds of the language are represented by letters. Typically, a child in this group needs to build understandings and skills in all three areas (Adams, 1990). The exit ticket for this group is the ability to sound and blend words with three sounds: a consonant sound, a short-vowel sound, and a consonant sound, taking advantage of the support that short-vowel word families provide. In order to achieve that goal, we plan direct instruction in letter names and sounds, in oral segmenting and blending, and in sounding and blending both individual phonemes and larger units. In addition, we build knowledge of a set of high-frequency words so that children can move into a variety of texts matched to their growing exploration of vowel sounds.

WHO NEEDS THIS INSTRUCTION?

Some children come to school with virtually no literacy knowledge. The explanation for this fact is usually a lack of experience (rather than a cognitive deficit). These children have not had the chance to learn concepts of print gradually through shared storybook reading (Justice & Ezell, 2002); they have not had the chance to develop initial phonological awareness through language play and rhyming (Neuman, Copple, & Bredekamp, 2000); they have not had the chance to develop initial letter-name and letter-sound knowledge through playful work with the alphabet (Ezell & Justice, 2000). The trick to serving these children is to give them fairly intense instruction as quickly as possible so that they can build the basic literacy understandings necessary to benefit from the regular curriculum. Based on knowledge of literacy development, we can predict three distinct sets of needs in this area. Figure 3.1 introduces them, and we describe each area in turn.

This most basic group is easily identifiable through informal assessments. If children cannot say the alphabet, they are good candidates. Additional data are unlikely to yield any diagnostic benefit. The "where to start" question is answered, "at the very beginning." It is important to understand that there is no child with literacy skills too weak to begin literacy instruction. For children who need to start at the beginning, targeted differentiated instruction is especially vital. We call instruction for these children "Basic Alphabet Knowledge."

A potentially larger (and more advanced) group is made up of those children who know virtually all of their letter names and sounds in isolation, but are not using what they know to read or spell words. They still need work segmenting and blending phonemes orally, and they still need work sounding and blending individual letter sounds. These children typically use initial consonants to guess words rather than using all of the letters; vowel sounds are especially challenging. We call instruction for this group "Using Letter Sounds."

Children who need work with using letter sounds may score well on informal letter-name and letter-sound inventories or on measures of letter-name fluency. They will score poorly, though, on measures of nonsense word fluency, on timed or untimed tests of decodable words in isolation, or on developmental spelling inventories. They will score poorly on timed tests of phoneme segmentation and blending. In natural writing, they will tend to represent only initial or initial and final consonants when they spell unknown words.

The last group of children we plan for in this chapter are those who can blend individual letter sounds, but need to learn to use larger units. Their decoding will be fairly accurate, but labored, and their sight word vocabularies will be small. They will need intense work with consonant–vowel–consonant patterns in order to move from sound-by-sound decoding (*c-a-t*) to onset–rime decoding (*c-at*). We call instruction for this group "Using Letter Patterns."

These children will be identifiable by their strengths in letter names, letter sounds, and untimed decoding tasks. On timed decoding tasks, however, they may perform accurately, but too slowly to meet benchmarks. They will be able to segment and blend individual phonemes, but they may exert extensive effort to do so. On spelling inventories, they will often represent vowels with what developmental spelling researchers

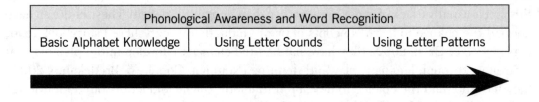

FIGURE 3.1. Potential targets for phonological awareness and word recognition.

call letter-name substitutions. This means that when they produce a particular vowel sound in isolation, as they are trying to spell a word, they may choose a vowel based on the fact that its name bears a phonetic resemblance to the sound they are trying to spell (Bear, Invernizzi, Templeton, & Johnston, 2008), perhaps spelling the word *bump* BOP. This may be because the child cannot use the short-vowel sounds to access the correct letter automatically. The letter names are often more easily accessible than the sounds. The child makes the short-vowel sound and then tries to decide which letter makes that sound. The letter sound for short *u* (which the child is trying to spell) bears a closer phonetic resemblance to the letter name for O than it does to the letter name for U. One of the goals for this group is to build automatic access to correct short vowels in spelling and automatic use of short vowels in decoding.

WHAT DOES THIS INSTRUCTION LOOK LIKE?

In planning demonstration lessons for all three of the groups we anticipate, we have drawn from instructional strategies typically referred to as direct instruction (see Carnine, Silbert, Kame'enui, Tarver, & Jungjohann, 2006, for a comprehensive description) and instruction that may be called word study (Bear et al., 2008; Ganske, 2000). We also use concepts derived from extensive practical research at the Benchmark School in Media, Pennsylvania (Gaskins, 2005).

Direct instruction is especially useful for basic skills work, when children must internalize and automate fairly low-level information so that they can use it later for higher-level work. Letter names, letter sounds, letter patterns, high-frequency words, blending, and segmenting are good candidates for direct instruction. You will see the influence of direct instruction in our lesson plans as we employ extensive teacher modeling, every pupil response with corrective feedback, and cycles of both new items and review items each day.

Word study procedures are useful for comparing and contrasting words based on their sounds and letter patterns. We draw on word study for initial sound sorting and for teaching short-vowel patterns. You will see the influence of word study in our lesson plans as we design activities in sets of related items, asking children to learn to compare and contrast sets of skills rather than focusing on skills in isolation.

You will see the influence of the Benchmark approach of fully analyzing words as we work with high-frequency words. Rather than rely on word walls to jog children's memory, we help children to internalize the sound and spelling of words by fully analyzing them—even when the letter-sound correspondences are irregular. In that way, we draw attention both to what is regular and to what is irregular about words.

In lessons for this group, we have a fairly small set of materials: Elkonin boxes with markers so that children can "say it and move it" (Ball & Blachman, 1991), letters (either on cards or made of plastic), picture cards, word cards, dry-erase boards, and alphabet strips. You will see that we do not use little books with this group. Their word recognition skills are too weak for decodable texts, and the use of syntactic and semantic cues to read predictable texts is inconsistent with our instructional focus on decoding. Teachers may choose to

Integrated	☐ In kindergarten and first grade, many teachers have alphabet strips, alphabet songs, letter cards, and picture cards that come with their basal curriculum. These can be used in differentiated instruction; they serve to make instruction coherent for children.
Explicit	☐ There are two and only two major areas of instructional focus; teachers work with oral phonological awareness tasks and with word recognition in isolation. ☐ Instructional talk is clear and brief; it targets only mastery of letter names, letter sounds, word reading, segmentation, and blending. ☐ The teacher names the focus skill or strategy. ☐ The teacher models the focus skill or strategy.
Scaffolded	☐ Group size is small enough to maintain attention. ☐ The teacher provides extended guided practice, with every student responding. ☐ The teacher corrects errors by modeling and repeating.
Systematic	☐ The teacher has a plan for a series of lessons for the group. Instructional strategies are the same each day, but there is both new and review content each day. ☐ The teacher has a plan for progress monitoring. At the end of a series of lessons, the teacher assesses whether each student mastered the content before regrouping and planning the next sequence of lessons.

FIGURE 3.2. Checklist for targeting phonological awareness and word recognition.

From *How to Plan Differentiated Reading Instruction* by Sharon Walpole and Michael C. McKenna. Copyright 2009 by The Guilford Press. Permission to photocopy this figure is granted to purchasers of this book for personal use only (see copyright page for details).

make one large set of materials, displayed in a pocket chart, for many of the instructional activities. For all three of our target groups, differentiated lesson plans are integrated with the work of the whole class, explicit in their focus on phonological awareness and word recognition, scaffolded directly by extensive and fast-paced practice with many trials, and systematically planned to meet specific goals. Figure 3.2 provides a checklist.

HOW CAN YOU PLAN THIS INSTRUCTION?

Conceptually, we have to search for a unique combination—the highest-utility instructional strategies and the most challenging instructional content that our group can handle. In making these choices, we use a developmental model to inform our thinking. We target the necessary alphabet knowledge (letter names and/or letter sounds) and then the most advanced oral phonological task that the group can process with support. For our Basic Alphabet Knowledge group, that task is initial sound matching. For both our Using Letter Sounds group and our Using Letter Patterns group, that task is oral segmentation and blending. Finally, we select a word recognition target. For our Basic Alphabet Knowledge group, that target is limited to high-frequency words; these children do not have the phonemic blending skills to decode words. Our Using Letter Sounds group will work with high-frequency words and also sound and blend at the level of the phoneme;

our Using Letter Patterns group will use a larger-unit (word family) approach to decoding. Figure 3.3 summarizes our targeted choices for each of the three groups. Note that both initial sound matching and phonemic segmentation and blending are oral-only tasks; in sounding and blending, by contrast, children are looking at the letters in the words.

Next, for each group we must choose instructional items. Because we want our instruction to be targeted and its effects measureable, it is important that we establish a rationale for choosing items. The rationale is slightly different depending on the skills of the group, so we describe each one in turn.

Planning for the Basic Alphabet Knowledge Group

For our Basic Alphabet Knowledge group, we are starting from scratch; at first, we really do not have diagnostic data to guide us. Therefore, we commit to teaching the alphabet directly, as a complete set, and to developing knowledge of a set of letter names in isolation. You will notice that we have planned to teach only the letter names in the first set of lesson plans we present in Appendix 3.1; when we are successful with the names we will then target the sounds. We have two choices to guide our selection of which letters

	Basic Alphabet Knowledge	**Using Letter Sounds**	**Using Letter Patterns**
	These children need to learn their letters and sounds.	These children need to use letter sounds to decode words.	These children need to use short-vowel patterns to decode words.
Alphabet	✓		
Concepts of Print	✓		
Letter Names	✓		
Letter Sounds	✓		
Initial Sound Matching	✓		
Phonemic Segmentation and Blending		✓	✓
Sounding and Blending Phonemes		✓	
Sounding and Blending Onsets and Rimes			✓
High-Frequency Words	✓	✓	✓

FIGURE 3.3. Choosing an instructional focus.

to teach. We can either teach them in the order of their frequency or we can teach them in the order established in the kindergarten curriculum (likely based at least partially on frequency). In the area of phonological awareness, we work with initial sound matching, a rudimentary phonemic segmentation task. To unify the lesson for the children, we target initial sounds to match our letter-name instruction. In practical terms, this means that the only important instructional choices teachers will make are which letters to teach and in what order. Again, since these children have so little literacy knowledge, we target high-frequency words in order of utility, simply choosing the 15 most frequent ones. Finally, in the area of concepts of print, we model fingerpoint reading with sentences that we compose each day. Figure 3.4 summarizes our planning choices. Note that these choices inform 3 weeks of daily lessons, 15–20 minutes each, with the final day reserved for assessments.

Planning for the Using Letter Sounds Group

For our next group, Using Letter Sounds, we must be more strategic in our planning. We need not waste time with alphabet work; this group can sing, say, and finger-point the alphabet. We also need not teach letter names and sounds in isolation; again, they have near mastery of these. Rather, we teach any unknown letter sounds in the context of sounding and blending consonant–vowel–consonant words. To facilitate sounding and blending, we first do oral phonemic segmentation exercises. Because the sounding and blending tasks will be scaffolded in two ways (by direct teacher modeling and by phonemic segmentation of spoken words and blending of spoken sounds), we choose difficult contrasts, addressing all five short vowels in just 3 weeks. As with our first group, we work on high-frequency words, but this time we will use a sight word inventory to select them. Any sight word unknown by any one member of the group will be taught to all. In this way, each child will be reviewing some known words and learning some new ones.

Parts of the Lesson	Rationale for Instructional Items	Actual Instructional Items
Alphabet	Knowing the entire set of letter names makes learning the individual names and shapes easier	Alphabet song Alphabet strips
Matching Initial Sounds	Matched to letter names	Words likely to be familiar to the children
Individual Letter Names	Either by frequency or to match the kindergarten curriculum; we begin with two letters and then add one each day	B, M, S, R, N, T G, I, P, A, H L, C, F, D
High-Frequency Words	Either by frequency or to match the kindergarten curriculum; we begin with two words, and then add one each day	the, of, and, a, to, in is, you, that, it, he was, for, on, are
Concepts of Print	Simple sentences containing at least one two-syllable word	

FIGURE 3.4. Planning lessons to develop basic alphabet knowledge.

Parts of the Lesson	Rationale for Instructional Items	Actual Instructional Items
Oral Segmenting and Blending	Matched to sounding and blending	
Sounding and Blending	Consonant–vowel–consonant words contrasting two short vowels each day; five new items for each vowel each day	short /a/, short /o/, short /i/ short /i/, short /u/, short /e/ short /a/, short /e/, short /i/
High-Frequency Words	Selected from results of high-frequency word inventory	Eight words per week

FIGURE 3.5. Planning lessons to develop use of letter sounds.

With this combination in mind, we target two new words each day, along with a review of previously taught ones, with a cumulative review every 5 days. Figure 3.5 summarizes our planning choices. Note that the most important task for the teacher is to decide which short vowels to compare and contrast each day and each week.

Planning for the Using Letter Patterns Group

For our final group, Using Letter Patterns, our target is to go beyond sound-by-sound decoding to work with larger units. Children do this when they begin to see vowel patterns; rather than sounding and blending each sound in a three-phoneme word, they see the vowel and what comes after it as a unit, blending an initial consonant sound with that short-vowel pattern. To facilitate this transition, we select vowel patterns to compare and contrast; this can be done simply by targeting high-frequency patterns rather than by relying on a diagnostic inventory. We work first with oral segmentation and blending at the phoneme level and then progress to work at the onset-rime level. The items we have targeted below are all high-frequency vowel patterns identified by Wylie and Durrell (1970). Instruction directs the children to listen for the difference in sound and to both read and spell the sound with a vowel pattern. As with our previous group, high-frequency word instruction is diagnostic in nature, with items taken from the results of high-frequency word inventories. Figure 3.6 summarizes our choices.

Parts of the Lesson	Rationale for Instructional Items	Actual Instructional Items
Oral Segmenting and Blending	Matched to letter patterns	
Teaching Letter Patterns	Sets of high-utility word families, three families per day, with five items in each	-at, -an, -ag, -ad, -ap -ill, -in, -ing, -ip, -it -ock, -op, -ot, -ug, -ick
High-Frequency Words	Selected from results of high-frequency word inventory	

FIGURE 3.6. Planning lessons to develop use of letter patterns.

STRATEGIES FOR EVERY PUPIL RESPONSE

Because we have targeted challenging content each day, our lessons demand extensive modeling and corrective feedback. To maximize both attention and practice, we employ a variety of every-pupil-response techniques. In our model lessons, included in Appendix 3.1, you will see teaching scripts that include every pupil response. Figure 3.7 describes the every-pupil-response techniques we have used for building phonological awareness and word recognition. Over time, teachers can mix their every-pupil-response techniques. Time spent in small groups is more valuable when students are participating the whole time. Because there are few students in a group, there is no reason for them to take turns responding during instruction.

TAKING STOCK

Recall the cognitive model we summarized in Chapter 2. If you have students whose needs extend back to phonological awareness and word recognition, they are likely to fall into one of our three sample groups: Basic Alphabet Knowledge, Using Letter Sounds, or Using Letter Patterns. We invite you to orient yourself to differentiated reading instruction by using one of our sets of lesson plans. Our goal, though, is to support your own

Technique	Description	Planning Necessary
Choral Echo Response	The teacher actually models each item, with all students repeating together.	Establish a signal for when the students will listen and when they will respond.
Finger-Pointing	Students respond by touching an item.	Prepare individual response charts.
Physical Gestures	The teacher uses a physical motion, such as counting with the fingers of the left hand, to direct children to say individual words or sounds.	Practice to make the motion fluid; consider using a prop, such as a Slinky.
Elkonin Boxes	Both the teacher and the students move markers into boxes to signify individual phonemes.	Prepare reusable boxes, on card stock or laminated, for two-, three-, and four-phoneme words.
Oral Choral Spelling	Children find a word and spell the word aloud; doing so forces them to focus attention on each of the letters.	Children need individual copies of the words targeted for the day.
Spelling	Rather than read words aloud, students spell them on dry-erase boards to demonstrate their letter-sound knowledge.	Develop procedures for writing quickly; avoid wasted time spent erasing.

FIGURE 3.7. Every-pupil-response techniques for phonological awareness and word recognition.

planning; the 42 model lessons we have designed do not constitute a continuous curriculum. If you have used any one of the three sets, you must still decide what to do next.

• For a Basic Alphabet Knowledge group, you must decide whether students need direct instruction in the remaining letter names or whether you can move to letter sounds. Use the assessment we have provided to measure students' response to this instruction. If they have approached mastery, redo the lessons, deleting the alphabet work, and instead teach both letter names and letter sounds. Use a high-frequency word list to plan new sight word instruction.

• For a Using Letter Sounds group, you must decide whether students need additional work with short-vowel sounding and blending or whether you can move to letter patterns. Use the assessment that we have provided to test whether students can sound and blend short-vowel words that they have not studied. If they can, move to letter patterns. If they cannot, choose new words and reteach.

• For a Using Letter Patterns group, you must decide whether students need additional work with short-vowel word families or whether you can move to the word recognition and fluency lessons described in the next chapter. Use the assessment that we have provided to judge whether students can generalize the patterns you have taught. If they can, consider lessons we present in the next chapter. If they cannot, choose new words and reteach. Use the results of your assessment to decide whether to reteach any high-frequency words; plan for new words based on your original inventory.

SUMMARY

Instruction for children who do not understand the utility of the alphabetic principle can be brief and systematic and quickly successful. We have anticipated three profiles for children in this group; there are no kindergarten children whose skills are too weak to begin here. Instruction here focuses only on attention to the sound structure of words (phonemic awareness) and attention to the relationship between that sound structure and the spellings of words. With targeted, supported direct instruction in this area, many children will be able to move quickly to a focus on word recognition and fluency, the topic of our next chapter.

Our goal is that you are flexible with your planning and thoughtful with your groupings. After every set of lessons, look for students who stand out, either as strong or weak performers. Those children might need to be moved to another group, whose skills are now better matched to their own. Every time you move a group or a child upward in our groupings, you have realized the potential of targeted, temporary differentiation.

LESSON PLANS

We have crafted lesson plans for each of these three groups. They begin with a generic script template, and then an example full script for the first lesson. What follows, then, is a set of new content for each of 13 additional lessons. Letters, word lists, and high-frequency words are numbered so that they can be photocopied, cut apart, collated, and used in actual instruction. You will see that we use a font that closely resembles children's handwriting to avoid confusion for the lower-case *a* and *g*. Occasionally, the number of words in a given lesson differs from the others. That is because we simply ran out of real words with the target features. In order to maximize challenge and practice, there will be some words whose meanings the children do not yet know. You will see that we do not build in time or scripts for vocabulary development. Our target for these students is squarely focused on word recognition. Finally, we have written assessments to provide feedback about whether the children learned the content covered in these lessons.

Basic Alphabet Knowledge: Generic Lesson Plan

Alphabet Review
We will start by singing our ABCs. The ABCs are the letters that we use to read and write. Watch my mouth and sing with me.
Now we will say the ABCs. The ABCs are the letters that we use to read and write. Watch my mouth. I'll say a letter, and then you say it after me.
We will see what the letters look like. There are two shapes for each one. I'll say the name, and then I'll point to the shapes. You say the name, and point to the shapes.

Initial Sound Sorting
We will work with sounds. You have a picture of a _____ and a _____. Point to the _____. The word _____ starts with the sound /_____/. Point to the _____. The word _____ starts with the sound /_____/. /_____/ and /_____/ are two different sounds. Now let's work with some other words. Say the word _____. Does _____ start like _____ or _____? _____ - _____ or _____ - _____? Point to the picture with the same starting sound.

Letter Names and Sounds
We will work with some letters. You have two sets of letters. These two _____ are named _____. Point to your _____s. Look at the shapes. These two are named _____. Point to your _____s. Look at the shapes. I will say a letter name, and you point to the right shape.

High-Frequency Words
We will work with some words. You have two words. The first word is _____. What word? You use that word when you say, " [common phrase]." The word _____ is easy to read. Watch me say the sounds. /_____/ /_____/; /_____/ /_____/. There are _____ sounds. Watch me write the letters: _____. There are _____ letters. The first letter(s) work together to make the sound /_____/. The next letter makes the sound /_____/. [etc.] Here is another word. I am going to say a word and you point to it.

Tracking Memorized Text
Here is a message I wrote for you. It says _____. You say that. Now let me show you how to read it. I look at each word, then I say the word out loud and touch it with my finger. Watch me. Now you do it with me.

Basic Alphabet Knowledge: Sample Script for Lesson 1

Alphabet Review
We will start by singing our ABCs. The ABCs are the letters that we use to read and write. Watch my mouth and sing with me.
Now we will say the ABCs. The ABCs are the letters that we use to read and write. Watch my mouth. I'll say a letter, and then you say it after me.
We will see what the letters look like. There are two shapes for each one. I'll say the name, and then I'll point to the shapes. You say the name, and point to the shapes.

Initial Sound Sorting: b/m
We will work with sounds. You have a picture of a ball and a moon. Point to the ball. The word *ball* starts with the sound /b/. Point to the moon. The word *moon* starts with the sound /m/. /b/ and /m/ are two different sounds.   Now let's work with some other words. Say the word *back*. Does *back* start like *ball* or *moon*? *Back-ball* or *back-moon*? Point to the picture with the same starting sound.   [Repeat with the rest of the words for lesson 1.]   (mother, my, box, man, big, make, baby, boy, more)

Letter Names and Sounds: Bb/Mm
We will work with some letters. You have two sets of letters. These two [indicate Bb] are named B. Point to your Bs. Look at the shapes. These two are named M. Point to your Ms. Look at the shapes. I will say a letter name, and you point to the right shape.   [Drill Bb and Mm]

High-Frequency Words: the, of
We will work with some words. You have two words. The first word is *the*. What word? You use that word when you say, "I see **the** moon." "I want **the** ball." The word *the* is easy to read. Watch me say the sounds. /th/ /e/; /th/ /e/. There are two sounds. Watch me write the letters: *t-h-e*. There are three letters. The first two letters work together to make the sound /th/. The last letter makes the sound /e/. Here is another word. This word is *of*. You use that word when you say, "I am tired **of** swimming." "May I have one **of** those markers?" The word *of* is easy to read. Watch me say the sounds. /u/ /v/; /u/ /v/. There are two sounds. Watch me write the letters: *o-f*. There are two letters. The first letter makes the sound /u/. The second letter makes the sound /v/. I am going to say a word and you point to it.

Tracking Memorized Text
Here is a message I wrote for you. It says [child's name] is a good reader. You say that. Now let me show you how to read it. I look at each word, I say each word out loud, and I touch it with my finger. Watch me. Now you do it with me.

Words for Initial Sound Sorting; Messages for Tracking

1	back, mother, my, box, man, big, make, baby, boy, more _____ is a good reader.
2	sale, big, move, by, sand, march, sack, bottle, Monday, soon, bark, me Today is _____.
3	red, bat, monkey, song, rat, Monday, sip, room, ball, mask, sandal, rock, me, bug, Saturday, bake _____ is a teacher.
4	top, sing, marker, tin, read, salt, milk, tan, round, soft, morning, ride, ten, muffin, send, run I like to do art projects.
5	tip, nest, rooster, town, ball, nice, room, bike, take, nap, ride, bark, rake, tear, bend, ripe, nose We can play on the playground.
6	neck, rat, gas, never, table, run, gift, nail, take, rubber, golf, knee, tap, rip, gap, tent My favorite story is _____.
7	sun, in, girl, nice, sick, if, goal, knock, sack, ill, game, knife, sock, iguana, go, no You are doing great work.
8	name, garbage, pack, illustrator, napkin, inch, geese, pail, imagine, peek, neat, indoors, garden, ink, gate, need, porch, ghost I ride the bus to school every morning.
9	if, absent, paint, rag, in, ill, ask, race, accident, pan, act, rain, important, radio, pig, pill, address We can draw pictures with our crayons.
10	hair, adventure, bear, macaroni, hot, after, alphabet, balloon, mad, book, hand, animal, meat, heart, backpack, market We do our best in school every day.

(continued)

11	tell, lift, horse, take, astronaut, let, tag, home, time, add, lock, ham, at, happy, top, ash, lake The children sang a song.
12	pig, cow, like, guy, lap, can, park, cap, gate, pot, left, give, pet, coat, lick, goalie This month we have _____ birthdays.
13	hand, forest, camp, lip, hit, castle, fork, loud, corn, horn, little, fat, cat, hot, fake, lake I went on a plane to visit my grandparents.
14	ham, down, ink, five, dive, hall, inch, find, hope, doll, ill, face, house, in, dog, feet We like to show what we know.

Student Materials for Initial Sound Sorting

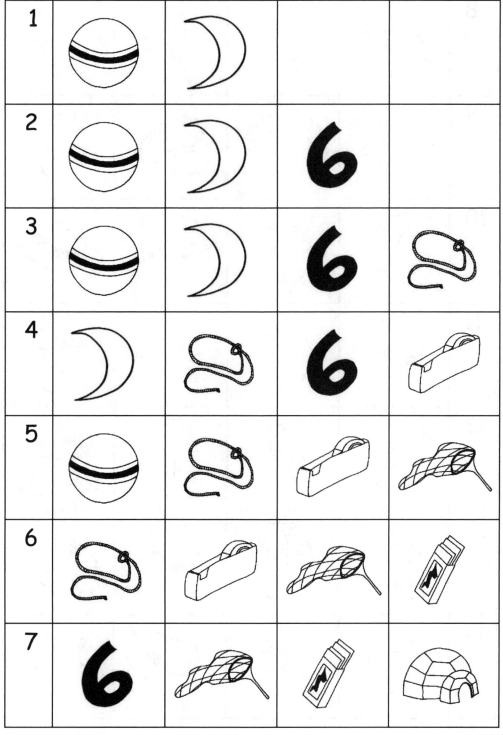

(continued)

Student Materials for Letter Names

1	Bb	Mm		
2	Bb	Mm	Ss	
3	Bb	Mm	Ss	Rr
4	Mm	Rr	Ss	Tt
5	Bb	Rr	Tt	Nn
6	Rr	Tt	Nn	Gg
7	Ss	Nn	Gg	Ii

(continued)

8	Nn	Gg	Ii	Pp
9	Ii	Pp	Rr	Aa
10	Mm	Aa	Bb	Hh
11	Hh	Aa	Tt	Ll
12	Pp	Gg	Ll	Cc
13	Cc	Ll	Hh	Ff
14	Ii	Ff	Hh	Dd

High-Frequency-Word Materials
for Basic Alphabet Knowledge

1	the	of			
2	the	of	and		
3	the	of	and	a	
4	the	of	and	a	to
5	and	a	to	of	in
6	and	to	of	in	is
7	of	a	in	is	you

(continued)

8	the	in	is	you	that
9	in	is	you	that	it
10	and	of	in	you	he
11	to	the	is	of	was
12	in	of	that	you	for
13	he	was	for	it	on
14	you	was	that	for	are

Basic Alphabet Knowledge: Assessment

Student Name _____

<table>
<tr><td colspan="16">Alphabet Knowledge</td></tr>
<tr><td></td><td colspan="15">Student can sing the alphabet.</td></tr>
<tr><td></td><td colspan="15">Student can say the alphabet.</td></tr>
<tr><td></td><td colspan="15">Student can track the alphabet.</td></tr>
<tr><td colspan="16">Initial Sound Sorting</td></tr>
<tr><td></td><td colspan="15">Given a word presented orally, the student can find a picture with the same beginning sound.</td></tr>
<tr><td colspan="16">Letter Names</td></tr>
<tr><td colspan="16">Given letters presented in random order, the student can identify</td></tr>
<tr><td>Bb</td><td>Mm</td><td>Ss</td><td>Rr</td><td>Tt</td><td>Nn</td><td>Gg</td><td>Ii</td><td>Pp</td><td>Aa</td><td>Hh</td><td>Ll</td><td>Cc</td><td>Ff</td><td>Dd</td><td></td></tr>
<tr><td colspan="16">High-Frequency Words</td></tr>
<tr><td colspan="16">Given words presented in random order, the student can identify</td></tr>
<tr><td>the</td><td>of</td><td>and</td><td>a</td><td>to</td><td>in</td><td>is</td><td>you</td><td>that</td><td>it</td><td>he</td><td>was</td><td>for</td><td>on</td><td>are</td><td></td></tr>
<tr><td colspan="16">Tracking Memorized Text</td></tr>
<tr><td></td><td colspan="15">Given a memorized sentence, the student can fingerpoint read.</td></tr>
</table>

Assessment Materials for Basic Alphabet Knowledge

Bb	Mm	Ss	Rr	Tt
Nn	Gg	Ii	Pp	Aa
Hh	Ll	Cc	Ff	Dd

the	of	and	a	to
in	is	you	that	it
he	was	for	on	are

Using Letter Sounds: Generic Lesson Plan

Say-It-and-Move-It

First we will work with sounds. I am going to say a word. Then I am going to stretch the word. Then I am going to say it and move it. Then you are going to do it with me.

Sounding and Blending

Now we will work with words. I want you to sound and blend these words. The way that you do that is you look at each letter, make each sound, and then say them fast to make a word. I'll sound and blend each one, and then you'll do it.

Now that we've done them all together, I want you to sound and blend on your own. See how many of the words you can do in one minute.

High-Frequency Words (begin with five)

We will work with some words. You have five words. The first word is _____. What word? Watch me count the sounds in _____. There are _____ sounds. Now watch me write the letters: _____. There are _____ sounds and _____ letters in _____. [Do all new words in this way.] I am going to say a word, and you point to it. [Do all words repeatedly in this way.] I am going to say a word, and you find it and spell it out loud. [Do all five words in a random order.]

Using Letter Sounds: Sample Script for Lesson 1

Say-It-and-Move-It
First we will work with sounds. I am going to say a word. Then I am going to stretch the word. Then I am going to say it and move it. Then you are going to do it with me. My first word is *cat*. I'll say it slowly: /c/ /a/ /t/. Now I'll move a marker into a box for each sound. Watch me. /c/ /a/ /t/ *cat*. Now you try. Your word is *cat*. What word? Say it slowly: /c/ /a/ /t/. Now say it and move it. [Repeat for each word.] (big, cob, top, bad, bid, not, bag, rot, did, dip, bat, cab, fig, bob) [Use the word list, but do not show the words to the students.]

Sounding and Blending (short *a*, short *o*, short *i*)
Now we will work with words. I want you to sound and blend these words. [Give a copy of the day's word list to each student.] The way that you do that is you look at each letter, make each sound, and then say them fast to make a word. I'll sound and blend each one, and then you'll do it. /c/ /a/ /t/ *cat*. You try. [Repeat for each word.] (cat, big, cob, top, bad, bid, not, bag, rot, did, dip, bat, cab, fig, bob) Now that we've done them all together, I want you to sound and blend on your own. See how many of the words you can do in one minute.

High-Frequency Words (begin with five)
[Since this part of the lesson depends on the words that the children do not know, there are no word lists provided. Refer to the materials provided for the Basic Alphabet Knowledge lessons for a more concrete example.] We will work with some words. You have five words. The first word is _____. What word? Watch me count the sounds in _____. There are _____ sounds. Now watch me write the letters: _____. There are _____ sounds and _____ letters in _____. I am going to say a word, and you point to it. I am going to say a word, and you find it and spell it out loud.

Words for Say-It-and-Move-It and Sounding and Blending

1	cat	big	cob	top	bad
	bid	not	bag	rot	did
	dip	bat	cab	fig	bob

2	rat	hop	jog	lit	jam
	hit	pot	sit	tap	lap
	pig	hid	rob	mat	pop

3	not	sag	hot	fit	zip
	jab	mom	hat	nip	cab
	pop	not	fin	dad	wig

4	mad	mop	bit	sob	rim
	rag	in	lot	tan	fat
	lip	dot	pad	rig	Tom

5	lad	tin	got	sop	hip
	kid	ham	rap	lot	his
	yap	cat	job	dig	mob

(continued)

6	sip	bed	met	cup	bug
	get	sit	pup	pin	yes
	fun	pen	tin	it	tub

7	rib	red	hut	rug	pit
	him	beg	mud	dig	cut
	let	web	bin	bus	men

8	win	den	tip	set	tug
	bun	bet	if	fin	rub
	led	dim	vet	bud	up

9	fit	hem	rid	nut	hen
	gum	tip	peg	hit	run
	pet	wig	but	wet	dug

10	is	sum	hug	leg	big
	lit	wet	hid	hum	sit
	lug	bed	jet	sun	wed

(continued)

11	get	big	yes	can	dip
	cap	bid	sat	tag	lab
	did	ten	met	fig	pen

12	fan	lip	red	had	let
	web	lit	pat	pig	beg
	ram	hit	wag	hid	men

13	pan	bet	bit	tap	den
	lip	am	led	rim	has
	pet	rig	ran	in	set

14	lad	tin	hem	hip	kid
	ham	pet	hen	rap	his
	yap	peg	cat	dig	wet

Student Materials for Using Letter Sounds

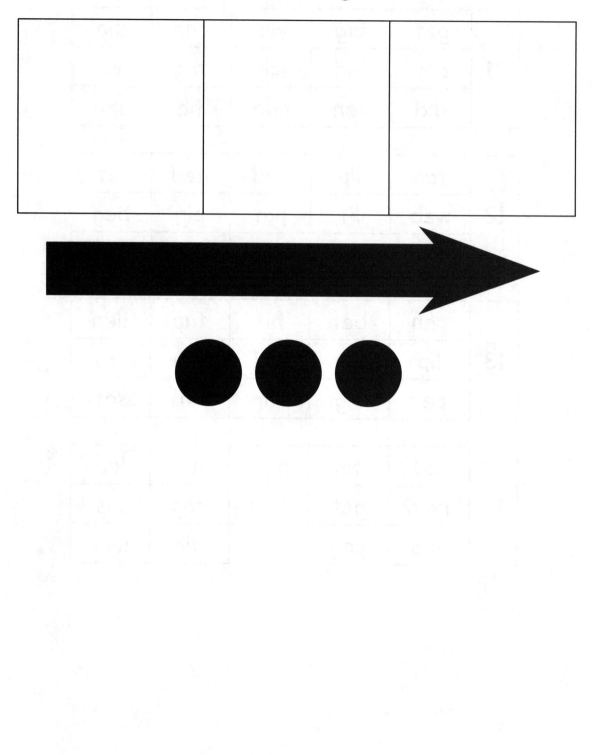

Using Letter Sounds: Assessment

Student Name _____

Segmenting and Blending							
Given words presented orally, the student can segment and then blend sounds							
map	net	sad	rim	mug	rip	cub	ten
Sounding and Blending							
Given words presented in random order, the student can sound and blend							
map	net	sad	rim	mug	rip	cub	ten
High-Frequency Words							
Given words presented in random order, the student can identify							

Using Letter Patterns: Generic Lesson Plan

Oral Segmenting and Blending
First we will work with sounds. I am going to say a word slowly and I want you to say it fast. Watch my fingers. Now I am going to say a word quickly and I want you to say it slowly.

Teaching Letter Patterns (-*at*, -*ag*, -*ap*)
Now we'll work on reading and spelling three vowel patterns. The /_____/ pattern is the sound at the end of the word _____. It is spelled _____. The /_____/ pattern is the sound at the end of the word _____. It is spelled _____. The /_____/ pattern is the sound at the end of the word _____. It is spelled _____. First I want you to listen to some words and tell me whether they sound like _____, _____, or _____. Point to the right sound. Now I am going to say the words again. This time I want you to spell each one. Use your patterns to help you.

High-Frequency Words
We will work with some words. You have five words. The first word is _____. What word? Watch me count the sounds in _____. There are _____ sounds. Now watch me write the letters: _____. There are _____ sounds and _____ letters in _____. I am going to say a word, and you point to it. I am going to say a word, and you find it and spell it out loud.

Using Letter Patterns: Sample Script for Lesson 1

Oral Segmenting and Blending
First we will work with sounds. I am going to say a word slowly and I want you to say it fast. Watch my fingers. /p/ /a/ /t/. Say it fast. [Repeat with all words.] Now I am going to say a word quickly and I want you to say it slowly. *Pat.* Say it slowly. Watch my fingers. /p/ /a/ /t/ [Repeat with all words.] (rap, sag, map, fat, nag, lap, mat, rag, rat, sat, nap, lag, wag, tap)

Teaching Letter Patterns (-*at*, -*ag*, -*ap*)
Now we'll work on reading and spelling three vowel patterns. The /at/ pattern is the sound at the end of the word *bat*. It is spelled *a-t*. The /ag/ pattern is the sound at the end of the word *tag*. It is spelled *a-g*. The /ap/ pattern is the sound at the end of the word *cap*. It is spelled *a-p*. First I want you to listen to some words and tell me whether they sound like *bat, tag,* or *cap*. Point to the picture with the same sounds. Your first word is *pat*. What word? *Pat-bat, pat-tag,* or *pat-cap*? Point to the picture with the same sounds as *pat*. *Pat* and *bat* have the same sounds. [Continue with the rest of the words.] (pat, rap, sag, map, fat, nag, lap, mat, rag, rat, sat, nap, lag, wag, tap) Now I am going to say the words again. This time I want you to spell each one. Use your patterns to help you. Remember that if you hear the /at/ sounds, the pattern is *a-t*. If you hear the /ag/ sounds, the pattern is *a-g*. And if you hear the /ap/ sounds, the pattern is *a-p*. Your first word is *pat*. [Dictate all words.]

High-Frequency Words
[Since this part of the lesson depends on the words that the children do not know, there are no word lists provided. Refer to the materials provided for the Basic Alphabet Knowledge lessons for a more concrete example.] We will work with some words. You have five words. The first word is _____. What word? Watch me count the sounds in _____. There are _____ sounds. Now watch me write the letters: _____. There are _____ sounds and _____ letters in _____. I am going to say a word, and you point to it. I am going to say a word, and you find it and spell it out loud.

Words for Using Letter Patterns

1	pat, rap, sag, map, fat, nag, lap, mat, rag, rat, sat, nap, lag, wag, tap
2	can, cat, lag, tan, mat, wag, man, rag, pat, nag, ran, van, rat, sag, fat
3	bad, cat, lag, lad, mat, nag, pat, dad, rag, rat, fad, sag, fat, had, wag
4	zap, dad, tap, wag, sag, had, rap, rag, pad, nap, nag, bad, lap, lad, lag
5	van, lap, ran, sat, nap, pat, man, sap, mat, zap, can, cat, rat, nap, tan
6	bill, bin, dip, tin, dill, hip, win, fill, rip, hill, sip, will, tip, till
7	sip, will, king, hill, tip, rip, fill, sing, dill, dip, hip, bill
8	zip, bit, win, fit, tip, tin, kit, bin, sip, lit, pit, rip, dip, sip, fin
9	pit, will, king, lit, hill, fill, kit, sing, fit, dill, bit, bill
10	tin, fit, king, win, lit, kit, pit, bin, sing, bit, tip
11	hot, cot, dock, got, hop, jot, lock, lot, sock, pop, mop, pot, mock
12	rot, dug, pop, hug, not, hop, mug, hot, rug, got, tug, cot, bug, top
13	sock, tug, wick, lock, mug, dock, dug, lick, rug, pick, hug, sick, bug
14	rug, pop, not, mug, rot, hop, hug, cot, tug, hot, dug, jot

Student Materials for Using Letter Patterns

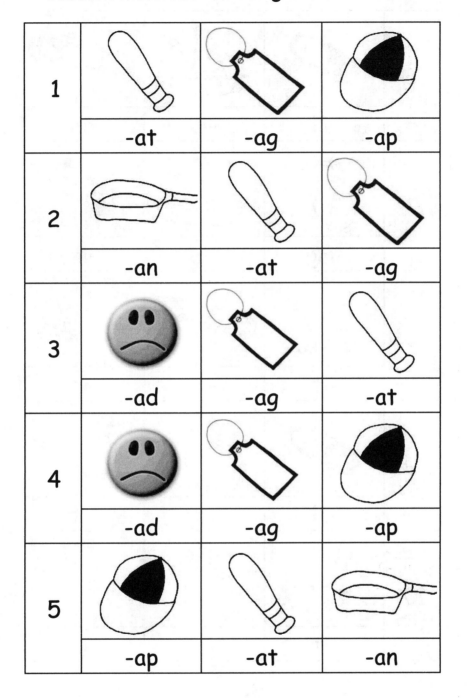

1	-at	-ag	-ap
2	-an	-at	-ag
3	-ad	-ag	-at
4	-ad	-ag	-ap
5	-ap	-at	-an

(continued)

From *How to Plan Differentiated Reading Instruction* by Sharon Walpole and Michael C. McKenna. Copyright 2009 by The Guilford Press. Permission to photocopy this form is granted to purchasers of this book for personal use only (see copyright page for details).

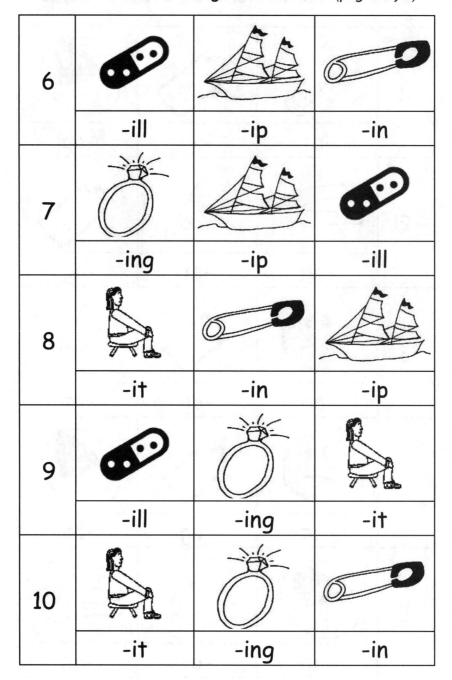

6	-ill	-ip	-in
7	-ing	-ip	-ill
8	-it	-in	-ip
9	-ill	-ing	-it
10	-it	-ing	-in

(continued)

11	-ock	-op	-ot
12	-ot	-op	-ug
13	-ock	-ug	-ick
14	-ug	-op	-ot

Using Letter Patterns: Assessment

Student Name _____

Segmenting and Blending							
Given words presented orally, the student can segment and blend sounds							
mad	bag	fan	map	hat	fin	lip	hit
top	pot	jug	tick	hill	wing	rock	
Sounding and Blending							
Given words presented in random order, the student can read these untaught short-vowel words.							
mad	bag	fan	map	hat	fin	lip	hit
top	pot	jug	tick	hill	wing	rock	
High-Frequency Words							
Given words presented in random order, the student can identify							

Chapter 4

TARGETING WORD RECOGNITION AND FLUENCY

Our next set of options for differentiated reading instruction is slightly more challenging—word recognition and fluency. You will see that we are moving, developmentally, from intense focus on phonemic awareness and decoding to coordinating skills and processes in the context of actual reading of text. Because our readers are novices in the alphabetic system, we use texts that facilitate their success by providing multiple decoding opportunities. We use repeated readings to make these opportunities more and more fluent. Our end goal is automatic word recognition in context.

WHO NEEDS THIS INSTRUCTION?

Children who can segment and blend orally and who also know their letter sounds and some short-vowel letter patterns may still lack the automatic sight word vocabulary necessary for true reading fluency. Decoding proficiency is not an end in and of itself. It is a means to an end. It may seem counterintuitive, but successful decoding of individual words and of words with related spelling patterns actually develops the deep, related links that readers use as they read virtually effortlessly—links between the phonology (the sounds of the words) and the orthography (the spellings of the words). On assessments, these children may do well on measures of phonemic segmentation and nonsense word decoding for short-vowel patterns, but still do poorly on oral reading fluency assessments because they have inadequate sight word vocabulary. They will be easy to identify with phonics or spelling inventories that move beyond short vowels; they will neither read nor spell long-vowel patterns reliably.

   Children who do not yet have the sight vocabulary they need for success in natural text tend to experience four roadblocks: (1) moving from consonant–vowel–consonant pat-

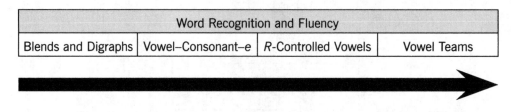

FIGURE 4.1. Potential targets for word recognition and fluency.

terns into patterns with more than one consonant (blends and digraphs), (2) understanding the basic principle by which long-vowel sounds are marked (vowel–consonant–*e*),
(3) understanding that vowels preceding the letter *r* have unique characteristics, and (4)
realizing that there are multiple patterns used to mark the same long-vowel sounds (long-
vowel teams). Figure 4.1 depicts this progression; we describe each more fully below. It
is important to consider that some children may need differentiated instruction in all of
these areas; they will start with blends and digraphs and need to move rapidly from one
focus to the next. Others may only need one or two of these issues to be addressed.

Our Blends and Digraphs group is generally moving from processing three units
to processing four or five. In some ways, this is only a matter of experience; many of the
instructional strategies we use will be the same ones that served our phonemic awareness
and word recognition group. In other ways, this is a more complex task. Blends can occur
either at the beginning or the end of words (e.g., *bl-*, *cr-*, *-st*, *-ft*). Blends are consonants
that are presented together but retain their individual sounds. For example, the word *sad*
has three phonemes (/s/ /a/ /d/), *sand* has four phonemes (/s/ /a/ /n/ /d/) with the final *-nd*
blend, and *stand* has five phonemes (/s/ /t/ /a/ /n/ /d/) with both the initial *st-* blend and
the final *-nd* blend. Blends are tricky in decoding because they add additional units to
be held in short-term memory; they are tricky in spelling because they are more difficult
to segment than individual consonants and vowels. Digraphs are not the same as blends.
They are tricky because they introduce new sounds not represented by individual consonants and they rob two letters of their more typical sound. In the word *ship*, for example,
the first phoneme /sh/ is not a blend of /s/ and /h/; it is an entirely new phoneme represented by two letters working together. Teaching that fact directly (rather than inviting
children to infer it) is fairly simple to do.

Our Vowel–Consonant–*e* group can handle the demands of four- or even five-
phoneme blending in short-vowel words, and they are ready to understand the first of
many long-vowel markers. The silent *e* is a fairly regular orthographic pattern. It is used
with all vowels, and there are relatively few exceptions. It is also a high-frequency pattern, so learning it will unlock many words. This group does not know that *cap* and *cape*
are two different words, and that the *e* at the end of *cape* signals that the *a* is long; that
realization is the target of their instruction.

Our third group, *R*-Controlled Vowels, also has a very specific set of patterns to
master. They need to learn that *ir*, *er*, and *ur* represent the same sound (the middle sound
in *bird* or *fern* or *turn*). They must also learn that the letters *or* make the sound heard in
torn, and that the letters *ar* make the sound we hear in *car*. *R*-controlled vowels pose a
challenge in spelling; there is no rule to tell which pattern to use (*ir*, *er*, or *ur*). However,

they need not pose the same challenge in reading. Rather, 3 weeks of practice decoding these patterns should allow students to read them correctly every time in every word; reading them correctly and thoughtfully in individual words may garner correct orthographic representations for the spellings of those particular words.

Our final group, the most advanced of the word recognition and fluency groups, is also learning concepts that are simple in reading but more complicated in spelling—Vowel Teams. Vowel teams include the following: short-vowel digraphs (*bread*), all of the two-letter spellings of the long-vowel sounds (*bait, boat, beat*, etc.), and diphthongs (/ow/ as in *cow* and *loud* and /oy/ as in *boy* and *boil*). Again, we target reading before spelling so that children can have successful experiences with words and gradually build up their store of correctly remembered, automatically accessed individual words. We choose to focus only on the long-vowel teams. We teach the teams that represent short-vowel sounds in the context of individual high-frequency words.

WHAT DOES THIS INSTRUCTION LOOK LIKE?

We will be drawing again on the direct instruction (e.g., Carnine et al., 2006) and the word study (e.g., Bear et al., 2008; Ganske, 2000) traditions. For this group, though, we will add two others: conscious attention to sound and spelling for building sight vocabulary (see Ehri, 1997, for a complete discussion), and the use of repeated readings for building automaticity (Samuels, 1979).

For these lessons, you will notice the influence of direct instruction in our insistence that the teacher actually model the decoding of every word presented in isolation for every lesson. Because of the modeling, relatively little time is wasted in providing corrective feedback to each child, one at a time. Rather, all children are more successful initially. In addition, the support that the modeling provides allows us to select a new set of challenging words each day. In this way, too, the teacher constantly supports the phonemic awareness skill of blending without devoting a portion of the lesson plan to oral-only work.

One way in which we differ from purer versions of direct instruction is that we do not match our decodable text to our decoding instruction with as much care. Direct instruction advocates might argue that every single word met in text has to have been taught first in isolation. We agree that there are readers with such weak skills that this becomes necessary, and they would need additional instruction in an intensive intervention. Remember that our target here is small-group instruction provided by a classroom teacher as part of a regular reading block. We assume that a vast majority of children, given targeted instruction to address an area of weakness, will be able to generalize that instruction to recognize all words with similar orthographic patterns. You will notice, then, that we do not spend planning time trying to make exact matches between the words in the word recognition parts of the lesson and the actual words in the decodable books. We use specific words to teach more general patterns found in many other words; we teach high-frequency words diagnostically because they all must be mastered and they all will be encountered many times over time.

Word study principles guide our selection of compare-and-contrast word lists. Rather than teaching only one specific orthographic element (e.g., digraphs) we choose words with digraphs and words with single consonants, in effect building on what the students already know to introduce new concepts. This allows us to reinforce content for those children who have just made the transition from the phonemic awareness and word recognition lessons to these more challenging ones. It also allows us to introduce our final (and most sophisticated) decoding strategy—decoding by analogy. When children decode by analogy, they isolate vowel patterns and then unlock them by consciously referring to words that they already know that contain the same patterns. One difference in our approach from purer word study work is that we are targeting decoding mastery rather than spelling.

Our focus on how to build sight vocabulary will be counterintuitive for many teachers. It is tempting to think that mature reading involves direct cognitive access from the spellings of words on a page to their meaning in memory, and that those spellings are processed as wholes. However, challenges to that intuition have a strong empirical and theoretical pedigree. Linnea Ehri has been a sage thinker and effective communicator for those striving to understand word recognition. She has described phases of word learning, in which individuals attend to different aspects of a word (Ehri, 1995). She has also proposed that sight word learning (both for phonetically regular *and* irregular words) comes from making connections between sound and spelling (Ehri, 1997). You will see her influence in both our decoding instruction and our work with high-frequency words. Not surprisingly, Linnea Ehri is one of the researchers who has contributed to the Benchmark School's curriculum, which we described in Chapter 3. We also use high-frequency words to engage teachers in showing children how specific words work.

In direct instruction, word study, and building sight vocabulary, children have repeated, supported exposures to the same words and to words with similar features. However, we take repetition one step further as we institute repeated readings of decodable text. We monitor time carefully in our lessons because we want children to have time to read and reread during the same instructional session (rather than reading the same text once each day for several days in a row). You will also see that we ask the students to read first alone, then with a partner, and then chorally—an instructional sequence exactly opposite the one that we recommend for our Fluency and Comprehension group (see Chapter 5). We do this because we want the children to read unknown words by decoding rather than by relying on short-term memory or pictures or meaning. Then we provide repeated readings with some support (in the form of a partner) and more support (in choral reading) so that children will experience multiple successful exposures to words, each more automatic than the last (Samuels, 1979).

Materials necessary for this group include word cards, dry-erase boards, Elkonin boxes, decoding-by-analogy anchor words, and decodable texts. By far the most challenging aspect of planning for this group is assembling adequate decodable text for children to use for reading practice. An ideal set of decodable texts to facilitate one set of 3-week plans includes 14 different decodables featuring the same phonics features. Many schools have established shared book rooms containing multiple copies of leveled books; we know of few who have shared libraries of decodable books organized by their phonics features. As with all libraries, the best course of action is to organize existing resources, identify gaps in the collection, and build resources over time. Figure 4.2 provides a list of decodable book series that we have found useful.

As teachers build libraries to support children's needs in word recognition and fluency, they will face resource issues. We agree with Jenkins, Vadasy, and Peyton (2003), who recommend that teachers create tables to describe the specific titles that they have for decoding practice. In a quick reading, a teacher could note the phonics elements that are featured *and* any difficult or irregular words that would have to be pretaught. This ounce of planning will prevent needless searching for a match of all phonics elements *and* all high-frequency word instruction. For our lessons, it is sufficient to identify books that correspond to specific orthographic elements. Figure 4.3 provides a basic template for building an organized library to correspond to our four types of lessons. Again, the goal is to identify at least 14 texts in each category and to note specific difficult words that would be easily pretaught in each one.

Before we begin to describe the actual planning process, we want to reinforce our call that this temporary, targeted instruction has four general characteristics. Like phonemic awareness and word recognition instruction, it should be integrated, explicit, scaffolded, and systematic. Figure 4.4 provides a checklist. Teachers who have committed to these general descriptive principles are ready to plan their lessons.

Series Name	Access Information
Reading A–Z	*www.readinga-z.com*
Educators Publishing Service Decodable Readers	*www.epsbooks.com*
Bob Books	*www.scholastic.com*
Flyleaf Publishing	*www.flyleafpublishing.com*
Phonics Readers Classroom Library	*educationalinsights.com*
Steck-Vaughn Phonics Readers	*steckvaughn.harcourtachieve.com*
The Wright Skills Decodable Books	*www.wrightgroup.com*
MCP Phonics and Reading Libraries	*www.pearsonschool.com*
Open Court Reading Decodable Books	*www.sraonline.com*
Scholastic Decodable Readers	*shop.scholastic.com*

FIGURE 4.2. Commercial sources for decodable books.

Title	Short Vowels	Blends	Digraphs	R-Controlled Vowels	Vowel–Consonant–e	Vowel Teams	Preteach

FIGURE 4.3. Template for organizing decodable books.

Integrated	☐ In first and second grade, many teachers have sound-spelling cards that are used in whole-group phonics instruction. In addition, many commercial programs come with sets of decodable practice materials. These can be used in differentiated instruction; they serve to make instruction coherent for children.
Explicit	☐ There are two and only two major areas of instructional focus; teachers work with word recognition in isolation and then students practice word recognition in the context of decodable texts. They do not use a guided reading format to do so.
	☐ Instructional talk is clear and brief; it targets only understanding the link between sound and spelling and procedural facilitation for repeated reading.
	☐ The teacher names the focus decoding skill.
	☐ The teacher models the focus decoding skill.
Scaffolded	☐ Group size is small enough to maintain attention.
	☐ The teacher provides extended guided practice, with every student responding throughout the lesson.
	☐ The teacher corrects errors by modeling and repeating.
Systematic	☐ The teacher has a plan for a series of lessons for the group. Instructional strategies are the same each day, but there is both new and review content each day.
	☐ The teacher has a plan for progress monitoring. At the end of a series of lessons, the teacher assesses whether each student has mastered the content before regrouping and planning the next sequence of lessons.

FIGURE 4.4. Checklist for targeting phonological awareness and word recognition.

HOW CAN YOU PLAN THIS INSTRUCTION?

Again, we are searching for maximum challenge in the instructional items, maximum effectiveness in the instructional strategies, and a brief and clear instructional delivery. This means that within the broad area of word recognition and fluency, we have to assign students to specific areas. Figure 4.5 aids in that selection by comparing and contrasting our four groups in terms of their skills. This time, though, the skills are more additive. In each successive grouping of lessons, all of the previous phonics features are reviewed while the new one is added to the mix.

The goal of the first set of lessons, blends and digraphs, is to extend the children's proficiency with short-vowel consonant–vowel–consonant (CVC) decoding (*mat*) to all short-vowel syllables: consonant–consonant–vowel–consonant (CCVC) (*chat* or *scat*) and consonant–vowel–consonant–consonant (CVCC) (*math* or *mast*), and consonant–consonant–vowel–consonant–consonant (CCVCC) (*stand* or *shift*). In week 1 we target initial blends, in week 2 we move to initial and final blends, and in week 3 we introduce the three most common digraphs (*sh, ch,* and *th*). Figure 4.6 provides an overview.

We employ basically the same set of instructional strategies to teach *r*-controlled vowel patterns. That is because, like blends and digraphs, *r*-controlled vowels are relatively simple to master through direct instruction and practice in sounding and blending.

	Blends and Digraphs	*R*-Controlled Vowels	Vowel–Consonant–e	Vowel Teams
Single Consonants	✓	✓	✓	✓
Sounding and Blending	✓	✓	✓	✓
Short Vowels	✓	✓	✓	✓
Consonant Blends	✓	✓	✓	✓
Consonant Digraphs	✓	✓	✓	✓
Vowel–Consonant–e		✓	✓	✓
R-Controlled Vowels			✓	✓
Vowel Teams				✓
High-Frequency Words	✓	✓	✓	✓

FIGURE 4.5. Choosing instructional focus.

It is important for teachers to know (and to explain) that these sounds are different vowel sounds from the short vowels they have been studying and that the vowel and *r* combine to represent one sound. To provide contrast, some of our words are not *r*-controlled. We have designed an "order" for introducing the patterns, but our choices are arbitrary; we simply tried to minimize confusion. We introduce the *r*-controlled patterns gradually over the 3 weeks; at first we focus on the three specific sounds (the sounds in *far, fir,* and *for*), with only one pattern (*ir*) representing the /ir/ sound; over the next 2 weeks we introduce the other two patterns (*ur* and *er*) that represent that same sound. Figure 4.7 represents our thinking. It may be slightly more difficult to match decodable texts to this particular progression. If the only texts that are available have *all three r*-controlled patterns, save them until the second week, using or reusing books with short vowels, blends, and digraphs during the first week.

Parts of the Lesson	Rationale for Instructional Items	Actual Instructional Items
Old Reading	Repetition builds automaticity.	The previous day's decodable book.
Sounding and Blending	All initial and final blends can be learned with attention to sounding and blending. The digraphs *sh, ch,* and *th* can be taught directly as two letters representing one sound.	Short-vowel words with initial blends. Short-vowel words with initial and final blends. Short-vowel words with initial and final blends and digraphs.
High-Frequency Word Instruction	Words selected from the results of a high-frequency word inventory ensure that the members of the group are building the sight vocabulary that they need.	Eight words per week.
Whisper Reading	Application of decoding and word recognition in even simplified text shows children that it is a facilitator of real reading; reading practice builds word recognition automaticity.	Any decodable text that includes short vowels and at least some words with blends and digraphs; the text need not be matched to the actual words practiced in the decoding phase.
Partner Reading	The use of a partner to listen (and to bear half of the decoding load) allows for an authentic purpose for rereading. The teacher can partner with one student each day, evaluating his or her decoding efforts.	
Choral Reading	Finishing each session with choral reading ensures that any decoding errors do not remain uncorrected, and ensures that the day's text is read at least once at an appropriate rate.	

FIGURE 4.6. Planning lessons for blends and digraphs.

Parts of the Lesson	Rationale for Instructional Items	Actual Instructional Items
Sounding and Blending	All *r*-controlled patterns can be learned with attention to sounding and blending. They can be taught directly as two letters representing one sound.	Words can contain blends and digraphs, and the *r*-controlled patterns are introduced in this order: *ar/or/ir* *ar/or/ur/er* *ar/or/ur/er/ir*
High-Frequency Words	Words selected from the results of a high-frequency word inventory ensure that the members of the group are building the sight vocabulary that they need.	Eight words per week.
Whisper Reading	Application of decoding and word recognition in even simplified text shows children that it is a facilitator of real reading; reading practice builds word recognition automaticity.	Decodable texts that have at least some *r*-controlled words.
Partner Reading	The use of a partner to listen (and to bear half of the decoding load) allows for an authentic purpose for rereading. The teacher can partner with one student each day, evaluating his or her decoding efforts.	
Choral Reading	Finishing each session with choral reading ensures that any decoding errors do not remain uncorrected, and ensures that the day's text is read at least once at an appropriate rate.	

FIGURE 4.7. Planning lessons to develop use of *r*-controlled vowels.

Our third potential focus in word recognition and fluency is vowel–consonant–*e* (VC*e*). The rule that when there is a final *e* the preceding vowel says its name is a fairly consistent and useful one; in fact it is one of the few phonics rules that we recommend teachers teach directly. It is important to tell children that the rule does not always work; high-frequency exceptions include *give, have, love, come,* and a few others. This is no reason not to teach the rule, however, because it is nearly always helpful with unfamiliar words. The general idea that long-vowel sounds can be marked with an additional letter is a good introduction to the more complex decoding that is to come. Because the final *e* is silent in these words, we use a letter-patterns strategy rather than sounding and blending. We also compare and contrast the VC*e* words with their short-vowel partners in order that children analyze each word for its pattern rather than simply responding with long-vowel decoding. We have decided to treat the long *U* sound in *flute* together with the long *U* sound in *cube*, even though the sounds are not exactly the same. Most children seem to be able to process both sounds easily, and it makes the 3-week plan more compact. Figure 4.8 presents our planning decisions.

Parts of the Lesson	Rationale for Instructional Items	Actual Instructional Items
Teaching Letter Patterns	The basic understanding that long vowels sound different than short vowels and that long vowels are marked with a silent e requires that students work with both short-vowel and VCe words.	Short a, aCe Short i, iCe Short o, oCe Short u, uCe All short vowels and all VCe patterns.
High-Frequency Words	Selected from results of high-frequency word inventory	Twelve words per week.
Whisper Reading	Application of decoding and word recognition in even simplified text shows children that it is a facilitator of real reading; reading practice builds word recognition automaticity.	Decodable texts that feature VCe words.
Partner Reading	The use of a partner to listen (and to bear half of the decoding load) allows for an authentic purpose for rereading. The teacher can partner with one student each day, evaluating his or her decoding efforts.	
Choral Reading	Finishing each session with choral reading ensures that any decoding errors do not remain uncorrected, and it ensures that the day's text is read at least once at an appropriate rate.	

FIGURE 4.8. Planning lessons to develop use of vowel–consonant–*e*.

Our last potential word recognition and fluency group can read short-vowel, *r*-controlled, and VC*e* patterns, and will take the very last step in single-syllable decoding: vowel teams. Vowel teams include any pattern with two vowels working together to represent one sound; most (but not all) of these are long-vowel sounds. They also include *y* and *w* acting as vowels. Because the patterns are more numerous than in our other lessons, we plan 6 weeks of instruction instead of 3. In choosing the decodable texts each day, it is possible to use individual texts with only a few of the targeted patterns even though the decoding instruction includes all of them. Figure 4.9 describes our choices.

STRATEGIES FOR EVERY PUPIL RESPONSE

We build upon the every pupil response techniques introduced in the previous chapter (choral echo response, finger-pointing, physical gestures, Elkonin boxes, and spelling) and add three more. Figure 4.10 provides a summary. These response techniques, when mastered by children, maintain the brisk pace and constant engagement necessary for targeted instruction to succeed.

Parts of the Lesson	Rationale for Instructional Items	Actual Instructional Items
Decoding by Analogy	We have chosen the highest-frequency patterns for each of the vowel sounds. Lower-frequency teams will be taught in the context of high-frequency word instruction.	Long-*a* teams (*ai, ay, ei*) Long-*o* teams (*oa, ow, oe, o*CC) Long-*i* teams (*ie, igh, i*CC) Long-*e* teams (*ee, ea, ei*) Long-*u* teams (*ue, ui, ew*) Diphthongs (*ou, ow, oi, oy*)
High-Frequency Words	Selected from results of high-frequency word inventory. Because decoding by analogy is more complicated, we reserve less time for high-frequency word instruction.	Four words per week.
Whisper Reading	Application of decoding and word recognition, even with simplified text, shows children that it is a facilitator of real reading; reading practice builds word recognition automaticity.	Decodable texts that have a range of vowel teams.
Partner Reading	The use of a partner to listen (and to bear half of the decoding load) allows for an authentic purpose for rereading. The teacher can partner with one student each day, evaluating his or her decoding efforts.	
Choral Reading	Finishing each session with choral reading ensures that any decoding errors do not remain uncorrected, and ensures that the day's text is read at least once at an appropriate rate.	

FIGURE 4.9. Planning lessons to develop use of vowel teams.

TAKING STOCK

Success of lessons in word recognition and fluency is measured by how quickly groups of children and individual children master this content and can move to our next type of lesson. It may be that using a set of our model lessons provides you the support you need to understand this type of instruction. Once you have finished, though, you will have to decide what to do next. It may be that the grade-level instruction or the curriculum materials that you have used are successful in developing competence in one or more of these areas but not others. Be sensitive to evidence that you can move directly to a focus on fluency and comprehension.

• If you are teaching a Blends and Digraphs group, you will have to decide whether students can decode four- and five-phoneme short-vowel words and whether they need help with *r*-controlled or VC*e* words. Use the assessment we have provided to measure students' response to this instruction and also to decide whether to move to *r*-controlled or VC*e* words. If neither of those patterns provides a challenge, move directly to vowel

Technique	Description	Planning Necessary
Constant Time Delay	Children read a word first in their head, and then, with a cue from the teacher, read it aloud chorally. This procedure ensures that all children will attempt to respond on their own, without being influenced by children who might respond more quickly without the cue.	Children need individual copies of the words targeted for the day.
Whisper Reading	Whispering is not the focus of whisper reading. Whisper reading is reading aloud quietly to oneself, without listening to others or matching their pace.	Children need individual copies of the texts.
Partner Reading	Partner reading is a procedure in which individuals read aloud to a partner who is following along silently, alternating roles.	Children need individual copies of the texts. Teachers must quickly assign partners and teach procedures for how to sit, for how much text to read at a time, and for how to request support from the partner.
Choral Reading	Choral reading is a procedure in which a fluent reader "leads" a group of readers to read aloud at the same time.	Children need individual copies of the texts.

FIGURE 4.10. Every-pupil-response techniques for word recognition and fluency.

teams. Use the results of your own assessment to decide whether to reteach any high-frequency words; plan for new ones based on your original inventory.

• If you are teaching an *R*-Controlled Vowels group, you will have to decide whether students need additional work with *r*-controlled words and whether they need work with VC*e* or can move directly to vowel teams. Use the assessment that we have provided to test whether students can sound and blend *r*-controlled words that they have not yet studied. Also consider whether they need to work on VC*e* words. Use the results of your own assessment to decide whether to reteach any high-frequency words; plan for new ones based on your original inventory.

• If you are teaching a Vowel–Consonant–*e* group, you will have to decide whether students understand that short-vowel words and long-vowel words have different spellings. Use the assessment that we have provided to judge whether students can generalize the VC*e* pattern. If they can, move on to vowel teams. If they cannot, choose new words and reteach. Use the results of your assessment to decide whether to reteach any high-frequency words; plan for new ones based on your original inventory.

• If you are teaching a Vowel Teams group, you will have to decide whether students can read single-syllable words with the vowel teams you have taught. Use the assessment that we have provided to judge whether students can read words with vowel teams. If they can, they are through with decodable text and are ready to focus on fluency and comprehension. If they cannot, choose new words and reteach.

SUMMARY

Success in our word recognition and fluency group depends on the use of decoding skills and strategies to build sight word knowledge. Students begin this type of instruction with letter-sound knowledge and the ability to decode CVC words. We draw on developmental theories to anticipate that students in this group will struggle either with expanding their decoding to include blends and digraphs, understanding the special case of *r*-controlled vowels, focusing on the simplest long-vowel marker (silent *e*), or learning the more extensive set of vowel teams. Our instruction targets these skills directly, with a strong dose of practice, both of words in isolation and in decodable texts. We do not ask teachers to choose these texts based on the match between the specific words and our word lists. Our instruction is designed to promote generalization, so the decodable texts can be chosen simply based on their general characteristics. At the same time, we provide word-by-word instruction for high-frequency words that the children need to know. This combination allows children to build the sight word banks that they need in order to read more meaningful texts with fluency and comprehension. You will see these decisions reflected in the lessons we provide in Appendix 4.1.

Success in targeted, differentiated instruction comes from identifying a specific skill deficit through assessments, planning and delivering instruction that focuses very directly on that deficit, and then using new assessments to measure effects. In the lessons that follow, we focus intense attention on very specific decoding deficits and decodable texts so that children can quickly get beyond them and move on to natural-language texts.

LESSON PLANS

We have crafted lesson plans for each of these four groups. They begin with a generic script template, and then an example script for the word recognition instruction in the first lesson in each set. We cannot script the high-frequency word instruction, because it depends on which words your assessments identify. However, we have provided a sample in the first Blends and Digraphs lesson.

What follows is a set of new content for each of a series of lessons. Word lists are numbered so that they can be photocopied, cut apart, collated, and used in actual instruction. You will see that we use a font that closely resembles children's handwriting to avoid confusion for the lower-case *a* and *g*. In order to maximize challenge and practice, there will be some words whose meanings the children do not yet know. You will see that we do not build in time or scripts for vocabulary development. Our target for these students is squarely focused on word recognition. Finally, we have written assessments to provide feedback about whether the children learned the content covered in these lessons.

Blends and Digraphs: Generic Lesson Plan

Sounding and Blending

First we will work with words. All of these words are real words, but you may not know them all. I want you to sound and blend these words. The way that you do that is you look at each letter, make each sound, and then say them fast to make a word. I'll sound and blend each one, and then you'll do it.

Sometimes two letters work together to represent one sound. *S-h* represents /sh/; *c-h* represents /ch/; *t-h* represents /th/. If you think of those letters working together to represent one sound, you can still sound and blend.

_____

Now that we've done them all together, I want you to sound and blend on your own. See how many of the words you can do in 1 minute.

High-Frequency Words

We will work with some words. The first word is _____. What word? Watch me count the sounds in _____. There are _____ sounds. Now watch me write the letters: _____. There are _____ sounds and _____ letters in _____. To know this word, you have to think about how the letters and sounds work together. I'll show you. In this word, the _____ letter(s) represent(s) the _____ sound.
[Continue until all sounds and spellings are linked.]
I'll say a word and you point to it. I'll say a word and you spell it.

_____   _____   _____   _____

_____   _____   _____   _____

Whisper Reading

Our new book is _____.
It will help you to know these words: _____.
You will know many of the words, and you can sound and blend most of the words that you don't know. Whisper read, pointing to each word as you say it. If you need help with a word, look up and I'll help you. If you finish before the timer rings, go back to the beginning and see if you can read more quickly.

Partner Reading/Choral Reading

Please get into partner position and reread. Look at your partner if you need help with a word. If you finish before the timer rings, switch roles and start over. When the timer rings, we'll read the book together chorally. Think about how much easier it is to read the more you practice.

Blends and Digraphs: Sample Script for Lesson 1

Sounding and Blending

First we will work with words. All of these words are real words, but you may not know them all. I want you to sound and blend these words. The way that you do that is you look at each letter, make each sound, and then say them fast to make a word. I'll sound and blend each one, and then you'll do it.

b-l-a-b blab; *b-l-o-b blob*; *c-l-a-m clam*; *c-l-a-p clap*; *c-l-o-g clog*; *c-l-u-b club*; *c-l-i-p clip*; *f-l-a-g flag*; *f-l-a-p flap*; *f-l-a-t flat*; *f-l-o-p flop*; *f-l-i-p flip*; *g-l-a-d glad*; *g-l-u-m glum*; *g-l-o-b glob*; *p-l-a-n plan*

Now that we've done them all together, I want you to sound and blend on your own. See how many of the words you can do in 1 minute.

High-Frequency Words (start, more)

We will work with some words. The first word is *start*. What word? Watch me count the sounds in *start s-t-ar-t*. There are four sounds. Now watch me write the letters: *s-t-a-r-t*. There are four sounds and five letters in start. To know this word, you have to think about how the letters and sounds work together. I'll show you. In this word, the letter *S* represents the /s/ sound. The letter *T* represents the /t/ sound. The letters *AR* work together to represent the /ar/ sound. And the letter *T* represents the last /t/ sound. The thing to remember is that those two letters *AR* work together to represent /ar/.

The next word is *more*. What word? Watch me count the sounds in *more m-or*. There are two sounds. Now watch me write the letters: *m-o-r-e*. There are two sounds and four letters in *more*. To know this word, you have to think about how the letters and sounds work together. I'll show you. In this word, the letter *M* represents the /m/ sound. The letters *ORE* work together to represent the /or/ sound. That's the thing to remember.

I'll say a word and you point to it. I'll say a word and you spell it. [Each day two more words are added, with all of the week's words reviewed together.]

Words for Sounding and Blending

1	blab	blob	clam	clap
	clog	club	clip	flag
	flap	flat	flop	flip
	glad	glum	glob	plan

2	plod	plop	plus	plum
	slab	slam	slip	slim
	brag	brat	brim	crab
	crop	drag	drip	drop

3	drip	drum	frog	grab
	grid	grim	grin	grip
	grit	prop	prom	prod
	trap	flap	trip	trot

4	crib	trip	trot	scab
	scan	skim	skin	skip
	skit	smog	snag	snap
	span	spit	spun	step

5	stem	swim	swam	snip
	snap	spin	spot	stop
	stub	sped	gram	clod
	smug	scat	stun	slap

(continued)

6	blank	blast	blend	blink
	clamp	clang	clasp	clump
	fling	flint	gland	plank
	plant	plump	slang	slant

7	slept	sling	slump	brand
	craft	crank	crest	crisp
	crust	draft	drank	drink
	front	frost	grand	grant

8	grump	grunt	grasp	print
	prong	tramp	trend	trunk
	trust	scalp	scamp	skunk
	spank	spend	spunk	spent

9	stamp	stand	sting	stink
	stomp	stump	stung	stunt
	swept	swift	swing	swung
	drift	crisp	skid	blab

10	clam	flag	glad	plum
	brim	crop	draft	tramp
	skunk	prod	grump	blast
	crest	slug	slip	blimp

(continued)

11	chap	chip	chop	chum
	shed	ship	shot	shut
	than	then	this	thin
	thud	chat	chin	shop

12	clash	flash	flesh	flush
	slush	mesh	crash	crush
	fresh	trash	smash	swish
	chant	chest	chimp	chomp

13	chunk	shut	shaft	shelf
	shift	that	them	thud
	thump	mash	much	munch
	bunch	hunch	crunch	lunch

14	plump	thank	think	grand
	blend	brush	flash	flank
	trash	spend	clink	blush
	blast	limp	hump	trump

Blends and Digraphs: Assessment

Student Name _____

Sounding and Blending				
Student can read these words with initial blends.				
slip	plan	smog	skin	blob
Student can read these words with initial digraphs.				
chop	ship	thin	chat	shot
Student can read these words with initial and final blends and digraphs.				
chunk	trust	slink	clamp	chest
High-Frequency Words				
Student can read these high-frequency words				
Decodable Text Reading				
Student can read with _____ accuracy in _____ seconds.				

A little boy went to camp. The sun was hot. The boy said, "I want to swim in a pond." He went to the pond. The pond had frogs. The frogs wanted to swim too. The boy and the frogs swam in the pond. Then they all sat in the sun and felt glad. The frogs went back to the pond. The boy went back to his tent. Then he shut the flap and went to sleep. The next day, the sun was hot. The boy went back to the pond to swim. The boy and the frogs were happy. (100 words)

R-Controlled Vowels: Generic Lesson Plan

Sounding and Blending

First we will work with words. I want you to sound and blend these words. The way that you do that is you look at each letter, make each sound, and then say them fast to make a word. Sometimes two letters work together to make one sound.

A-r represents /ar/; *o-r* represents /or/; *i-r* represents /ur/; *u-r* represents /ur/; *e-r* represents /er/.

If you think of those letters working together to represent one sound, you can still sound and blend. I'll do them first, and then we'll do them together.

_____

Now that we've done them all together, I want you to sound and blend on your own. See how many of the words you can do in 1 minute.

High-Frequency Words

We will work with some words. The first word is _____. What word? Watch me count the sounds in _____. There are _____ sounds. Now watch me write the letters: _____. There are _____ sounds and _____ letters in _____. To know this word, you have to think about how the letters and sounds work together. I'll show you. In this word, the _____ letter(s) represent(s) the _____ sound.

[Continue until all sounds and spellings are linked.]

I'll say a word and you point to it. I'll say a word and you spell it.

_____   _____   _____   _____

_____   _____   _____   _____

Whisper Reading

Our new book is _____.

It will help you to know these words: _____.

You will know many of the words, and you can sound and blend most of the words that you don't know. Whisper read, pointing to each word as you say it. If you need help with a word, look up and I'll help you. If you finish before the timer rings, go back to the beginning and see if you can read more quickly.

Partner Reading/Choral Reading

Please get into partner position and reread. Look at your partner if you need help with a word. If you finish before the timer rings, switch roles and start over. When the timer rings, we'll read the book together chorally. Think about how much easier it is to read the more you practice.

Words for Sounding and Blending

1	arch	pork	cord	firm
	arm	born	bird	first
	art	form	fir	girl
	card	corn	dirt	sir

2	barb	spark	cork	sir
	bark	fork	nor	skirt
	dark	horse	third	chirp
	dart	north	swirl	thirst

3	shark	force	north	stir
	march	ford	short	squirt
	harp	forth	birch	thirst
	car	horn	birth	twirl

4	scarf	yard	fort	squirm
	charm	port	horn	shirt
	chart	porch	stork	whirl
	lark	storm	thorn	fir

5	lark	harm	torn	stir
	smart	scorn	worn	first
	start	sort	torch	skirt
	hard	sport	sworn	dirt

(continued)

6	cart	fern	or	blur
	park	germ	score	blurt
	starve	jerk	shore	burn
	part	term	store	burp

7	jar	perch	more	burst
	snarl	nerve	tore	church
	tart	stern	chore	churn
	yarn	verse	pore	curb

8	barge	clerk	swore	curl
	far	perk	wore	curve
	large	merge	porch	fur
	sharp	verb	forth	hurl

9	scar	nerd	north	lurk
	harm	term	short	nurse
	farm	perch	worn	purse
	charm	stern	scorn	spur

10	chart	herd	port	spurt
	march	verb	sport	surf
	hard	nerve	score	surge
	spar	verse	core	turf

(continued)

11	mart	perch	stir	turn
	mark	perk	firs	purr
	parts	nerve	pork	turf
	lard	bird	port	spur

12	marsh	verse	third	surf
	tarts	firm	sort	urn
	start	squirt	sore	curb
	merge	shirt	sports	hurt

13	spark	stern	skirt	nurse
	barb	clerk	twirl	purge
	harsh	jerk	sort	purse
	terms	ferns	dorm	turns

14	farms	germs	flirt	spurt
	charm	terms	born	slur
	dark	birch	thorn	blur
	spark	first	fork	blurt

R-Controlled Vowels: Assessment

Student Name _____

Sounding and Blending				
Student can read these words with initial blends.				
chart	term	skirt	north	burn
spark	verse	firm	porch	purse
High-Frequency Words				
Student can read these high-frequency words.				
Decodable Text Reading				
Student can read with _____ accuracy in _____ seconds.				

It is fun to play sports. I wanted to play soccer. First, I went to the store to get a shirt and a ball. I went to the park to kick the ball far. It was hard. I fell in the dirt and my arm was sore. Then a girl helped me. She was a soccer star. We started to play. She helped me kick the ball far. She helped me to score. She helped me to turn and kick. We got thirsty, so we drank some water. Then we played some more. When it got dark, we went home. (100 words)

Vowel-Consonant-*e*: Generic Lesson Plan

Teaching Letter Patterns

First we will work with word patterns. We are going to start by listening for long- and short-vowel sounds. Remember that a long vowel says its name. We are going to review words that have the vowel sounds in_____. Stretch those words with me so that we can find the vowel sounds.
I'll say a word and you point to the right vowel sound.

_____

When you see a final *e*, the vowel says its name. I'll say a word. I want you to find the word, and then when I say "go," spell it out loud.
[Or]
I will say a word, and I want you to spell it on your white board. Remember to use a final *e* when the vowel says its name.

High-Frequency Words

We will work with some words. The first word is _____. What word? Watch me count the sounds in _____. There are _____ sounds. Now watch me write the letters: _____. There are _____ sounds and _____ letters in _____. To know this word, you have to think about how the letters and sounds work together. I'll show you. In this word, the _____ letter(s) represent(s) the _____ sound.
[Continue until all sounds and spellings are linked.]
I'll say a word and you point to it. I'll say a word and you spell it.

_____   _____   _____   _____

_____   _____   _____   _____

Whisper Reading

Our new book is _____.
It will help you to know these words: _____.
You will know many of the words, and you can sound and blend most of the words that you don't know. Whisper read, pointing to each word as you say it. If you need help with a word, look up and I'll help you. If you finish before the timer rings, go back to the beginning and see if you can read more quickly.

Partner Reading/Choral Reading

Please get into partner position and reread. Look at your partner if you need help with a word. If you finish before the timer rings, switch roles and start over. When the timer rings, we'll read the book together chorally. Think about how much easier it is to read the more you practice.

Vowel-Consonant-*e*: Sample Script for Lesson 1

Teaching Letter Patterns

First we will work with word patterns. We are going to start by listening for long- and short-vowel sounds. Remember that a long vowel says its name. We are going to review words that have the vowel sounds in *hat, cake, pig,* and *bike*. Stretch those words with me so that we can find the vowel sounds: *h-a-t; p-i-g; c-a-k; b-i-k*

I'll say a word and you point to the right vowel sound. Your first word is *mad*. Point to the word with the same vowel sound. Right. *Mad* has the same sound as *hat*. The next word is *ape*. Point to the word with the same vowel sound. *Ape* has the same sound as *cake*. [Finish all of the words.]

_____

[Distribute the word lists.]
When you see a final *e*, the vowel says its name. I'll say a word. I want you to find the word, and then when I say "go," spell it out loud.
[Or]
I will say a word, and I want you to spell it on your white board. Remember to use a final *e* when the vowel says its name.

Words for Teaching Letter Patterns

1	mad	ape	bake	chat
	cane	rag	dive	lift
	dime	line	flat	brim

2	cave	dime	past	chip
	strap	fame	drive	mask
	milk	fine	link	game

3	rake	slam	dash	print
	lime	lace	like	shift
	lip	nice	math	wave

4	drag	pipe	fake	pink
	fade	pine	skin	task
	fist	past	size	grade

5	broke	chap	flake	grip
	stand	close	snap	fig
	trim	lake	space	code

6	cute	home	crop	gum
	dome	shop	cone	huge
	pot	fume	mud	mule

(continued)

7	use	pot	hose	dune
	spot	hope	duke	poke
	blush	huge	nod	jug

8	rude	dump	rode	dusk
	phone	tune	rule	much
	drop	chop	strut	those

9	flute	prune	chose	skunk
	note	shop	flop	tube
	pond	stun	stone	shot

10	crush	trot	rope	kid
	robe	tune	mop	stove
	June	blot	prune	hum

11	dust	bash	drove	drink
	nine	flame	list	plop
	froze	mile	mute	date

12	romp	wife	shake	mint
	safe	mole	risk	wide
	lamp	rule	lone	bunk

(continued)

13	smoke	slot	five	spruce
	spike	tape	vote	club
	blink	plant	state	spin

14	shape	swam	fish	hive
	poke	place	life	sob
	sift	dome	tune	trust

Student Materials for Teaching Letter Patterns

__a__	__i__	__o__	__u__
__a__e	__i__e	__o__e	__u__e

Vowel-Consonant-*e*: Assessment

Student Name _____

Letter Patterns				
Student can listen to these words and tell whether they have long or short sounds.				
pack	ice	place	cute	lid
rug	stand	stun	tame	pot
shift	plume	time	pond	vote

Student can spell these words correctly.			
cap	cape	man	mane
hop	hope	hat	hate
bit	bite	fat	fate

High-Frequency Words				
Student can read these high-frequency words.				

Decodable Text Reading
Student read with _____ accuracy in _____ seconds.
It was time for the big bike race. Mike and Jen were set to ride. They had to ride five miles. It was hot, so they had lots of water. When the race started, Mike was the first to glide down the hill. Then Jen came close. She rode past Mike. She rode fast, but she was still safe. She rode past a lake. She rode for miles. Mike came after her, but she was fast. Jen made it to the line first. Mike came next. Jen and Mike were tired. They sat under a tree and took a rest. (100 words)

Long-Vowel Teams: Generic Lesson Plan

Decoding by Analogy

You know how to read short vowels, *r*-controlled vowels, and vowel–consonant-*e* patterns. We are going to work with other long-vowel patterns. The way we'll do it is we'll learn a set of clue words, and we'll use those words to read other words. Your clue words today are _____. They all use patterns to spell the long _____. In the word _____, the letters _____ represent the long _____.

I am going to show you a new word. I want you to point to our clue word with the same pattern and then say

"I know_____. This must be _____."

Let's see how many times you can read all of your new words in 1 minute.
Let's review one of our old lists. How many times can you read these words?

High-Frequency Words

We will work with some words. The first word is _____. What word? Watch me count the sounds in _____. There are _____ sounds. Now watch me write the letters: _____. There are _____ sounds and _____ letters in _____. To know this word, you have to think about how the letters and sounds work together. I'll show you. In this word, the _____ letter(s) represent(s) the _____ sound.
[Continue until all sounds and spellings are linked.]
I'll say a word and you point to it. I'll say a word and you spell it.

_____ _____ _____ _____

Whisper Reading

Our new book is _____.
It will help you to know these words: _____.
You will know many of the words, and you can sound and blend most of the words that you don't know. Whisper read, pointing to each word as you say it. If you need help with a word, look up and I'll help you. If you finish before the timer rings, go back to the beginning and see if you can read more quickly.

Partner Reading/Choral Reading

Please get into partner position and reread. Look at your partner if you need help with a word. If you finish before the timer rings, switch roles and start over. When the timer rings, we'll read the book together chorally. Think about how much easier it is to read the more you practice.

Long-Vowel Teams: Sample Script for Lesson 1

Decoding by Analogy

You know how to read short vowels, *r*-controlled vowels, and vowel-consonant-*e* patterns. We are going to work with other long-vowel patterns. The way we'll do it is we'll learn a set of clue words, and we'll use those words to read other words.

Your clue words today are *rain*, *May*, and *eight*. They all use patterns to spell the long *A*. In the word *rain*, the letters *AI* represent the long *A*. In the word *May*, the letters *AY* represent the long *A*. In the word *eight*, the letters *EIGH* represent the long *A*. We are learning three different ways that the long *A* is spelled.

I am going to show you a new word. I want you to point to our clue word with the same pattern and then say

"I know_____. This must be _____."

Here is the first word [BAIT.] "I know rain. This must be bait." Continue with the rest of the words.

Let's see how many times you can read all of your new words in 1 minute.

Let's review one of our old lists. How many times can you read these words?

Words for Decoding by Analogy

1	bait	neigh	reign	stain
	bay	claim	play	ray
	weigh	way	maid	pain

2	drain	freight	stray	wail
	day	plain	nail	paint
	sprain	hay	say	sleigh

3	wait	gray	claim	vein
	jay	faint	weight	pay
	praise	slay	waist	reign

4	stay	chain	vein	eighth
	aim	clay	sway	main
	tray	tail	nail	hay

5	way	spray	paid	veil
	stain	freight	pays	claim
	sprain	train	stray	straight

6	boast	doe	folk	blow
	toad	road	bowl	roast
	bold	volt	oats	ghost

(continued)

7	moat	foe	soap	bolt
	flow	both	stroll	glow
	cold	flown	toast	foam

8	coat	comb	grow	low
	fold	oath	hoe	sold
	roast	gold	know	coast

9	host	scold	moan	growth
	goal	roach	toe	show
	mold	mow	jolt	float

10	coach	shown	woe	poll
	most	croak	slow	poach
	snow	post	groan	throw

11	bright	cry	child	blind
	bind	fight	spry	light
	spy	try	flight	why

12	spy	high	blind	climb
	cry	sky	light	bright
	knight	find	might	shy

13	right	dry	grind	sigh
	flight	might	fly	mind
	fry	hind	sight	find

(continued)

14	slight	pry	blind	wild
	rind	thigh	shy	knight
	sign	sky	tight	sight

15	light	sly	wind	why
	dry	fight	slight	knight
	grind	spry	light	blind

16	beach	brief	beef	keep
	screen	lean	read	greed
	flea	beast	field	sweep

17	eat	sleet	chief	least
	teeth	peach	leash	sweet
	speed	eel	mean	feed

18	bead	week	fiend	queen
	ease	grief	greet	cream
	yield	peace	east	jeep

19	beak	thief	flea	three
	niece	deal	speech	plea
	fleet	piece	feast	creep

20	heal	shriek	heap	keen
	priest	heat	reef	reach
	screen	shield	leave	sheep

(continued)

21	blew	clue	bruise	crew
	cruise	brew	suit	threw
	due	cue	chew	knew

22	dew	flue	juice	true
	bruise	few	suits	flew
	sue	glue	drew	crews

23	grew	hue	suits	shrews
	dew	knew	screw	chew
	true	cruise	mew	few

24	glue	cue	shrewd	bruise
	suits	shrew	sue	true
	stew	drew	juice	threw

25	news	knew	true	hue
	hue	strewn	grew	dew
	shrewd	glue	stew	cruise

26	boy	bound	void	clown
	boil	brow	wow	snout
	cloud	sprout	coil	cow

27	broil	coy	couch	crowd
	drown	toil	scout	south
	spout	down	spoil	crown

(continued)

28	coin	joy	crouch	soil
	count	clown	fowl	pound
	shout	point	doubt	brown

29	moist	soy	found	frown
	proud	loin	sound	gown
	foul	howl	how	joint

30	joy	grouch	plow	broil
	prowl	join	scowl	town
	round	ground	hoist	vow

Student Materials for Decoding by Analogy

Long-A Teams		
rain	May	eight
__ai__	__ay	__eigh__

Long-O Teams			
boat	toe	low	cold
__oa__	__oe__	__ow__	__o___

Long-I Teams		
high	my	kind
__igh__	__y	__i___

Long-E Teams		
eat	bee	chief
__ea__	__ee__	__ie__

Long-U Teams		
new	blue	fruit
__ew	__ue	__ui__

Owl/Oil Teams			
oil	toy	house	owl
__oi__	__oy	__ou__	__ow__

Vowel Teams: Assessment

Student Name _____

Letter Patterns				
Students can read these words correctly.				
shown	glue	field	blind	pray
bleed	stow	threw	weigh	climb
sleigh	stay	greet	thief	soak
high	tight	spy	shy	woe
juice	throat	most	fold	clue
leash	plain	stew	waist	heap
suit	soy	toil	cloud	growl
High-Frequency Words				
Student can read these high-frequency words				
Decodable Text Reading				
Student can read with _____ accuracy in _____ seconds.				
We went on a trip to the beach. We wanted to see the sea spray. We wanted to hear the sound of the waves. The sun was bright and the sea was green. We saw a boat blown by the breeze. We went for a swim, and stayed close to the shore where it was not too deep. Then we came out to get dry. We brought a pail so that we could play in the sand. We knew it would be cold in the night, so we found a spot to stay warm. It was a day of fun. (100 words)				

Chapter 5

TARGETING FLUENCY AND COMPREHENSION

Our differentiation "staircase" follows children as they progress toward proficiency. At the next-to-highest step, children possess considerable sight vocabularies and have mastered all or nearly all decoding skills. They are not automatic in applying these skills, however, and their ability to do so is the key to fluency. These children will benefit from reading connected text because doing so affords them practice in applying their word recognition skills. That practice is the foundation of effective fluency instruction.

It is useful to contrast these children with those who are still on the second step. These children have not yet mastered the full range of decoding skills. They need instruction in these skills before fluency methods are likely to be effective. This is because good fluency instruction assumes that such skills have been learned and that they simply need to be practiced until they can be applied automatically, without conscious effort. Children on the third stair step are in this position. They are poised to become fluent readers by practicing the word recognition skills they have acquired. This practice will take place in authentic texts at appropriate levels of difficulty.

Although fluency is the principal target for these young readers, comprehension also plays an important role. Some teachers have raised the objection that a focus on fluency leads to the creation of "word callers." Schwanenflugel and Ruston (2008) have found no evidence for such a fear. Nevertheless, we believe that the engaging texts used in effective small-group fluency instruction provide an opportunity to prompt inferential thinking about their content. We therefore reserve a few minutes at the end of each lesson, after two readings of a text segment, to foster such thinking.

WHO NEEDS THIS INSTRUCTION?

Figure 5.1 displays the characteristics of children who are most likely to benefit from small-group instruction that targets fluency and comprehension. The exit ticket for these children is the attainment of fluency benchmarks appropriate to their grade level.

Grade Level	Characteristics of Children	Small-Group Instructional Approach
1	Depending on the decoding curriculum and a child's rate of progress, some children may be ready for fluency work in first grade. This would depend on their having acquired a full range of decoding skills.	Children are given a chance to read texts that are challenging but comprehensible. These texts are neither decodable nor predictable books but represent authentic literature and information books.
2–3	Children have achieved benchmark levels in word recognition, making adequate progress in both decoding and sight word recognition. They are not fluent readers but have acquired a full range of word recognition skills.	

FIGURE 5.1. Children whose needs are best met through fluency and comprehension.

Remember that these benchmarks are moving targets. As children pass from first to third grade, they must both increase their reading rate *and* demonstrate it in more complicated texts. Movement to our most exclusive club—the top stair on our staircase—requires that each successive fluency benchmark be met. Failure to meet the next fluency benchmark along with evidence of adequate word recognition skills means that the child would be best served through fluency work during small-group time.

Most small-group work of this kind occurs in grades 2 and 3. In the latter part of first grade, it is possible that some children would be best served by a focus on fluency. However, this would depend on how extensive their decoding skills are. If they have not yet achieved a wide range of skills, but are performing at benchmark levels in decoding, their small-group instruction should target vocabulary and comprehension in a read-aloud setting. We describe this instruction in detail in Chapter 6.

For any child in the primary grades, the decision strategy represented in Figure 2.3 in Chapter 2 illustrates how a teacher would determine which type of group is most appropriate. As this figure indicates, children who are best served in the fluency and comprehension group have two characteristics: (1) they are not at benchmark in oral reading fluency and (2) they have acquired all, or nearly all, decoding skills.

WHAT DOES THIS INSTRUCTION LOOK LIKE?

Sets of trade books are the only instructional materials needed for this group, unless a teacher chooses to devote a few minutes to advanced decoding applications involving multisyllabic words. In a 3-week cycle, the number of books will depend on their length and complexity. Because the principal focus is fluency, teacher talk is minimal. Little time is spent preparing children for the book, and discussions are limited to prompting a few inferences and assisting the children in summarizing. The lion's share of time is devoted to oral reading and rereading of text segments because in effective fluency instruction the amount of time children spend actually reading is critical (Shanahan, 2006). This means that round robin oral reading, questionable under any circumstances (see Ash & Kuhn, 2006), has no place in these lessons.

The books themselves should be chosen to reflect the interests of children, with some attention to standards in English language arts, science, and social studies. The books should be similar in readability, targeting the end of the grade level taught. (For example, a second-grade fluency and comprehension group would read books written at a high second-grade level.) Although information books should be included, nonlinear elements (e.g., sidebars, tables, and figures) can complicate fluency work, and books should be chosen to minimize these features.

A typical small-group lesson begins with the teacher either quickly introducing a new book or assisting students in producing a quick oral summary of the current book, up to the point where reading left off. The teacher next identifies the text segment to be read that day. This segment is read twice by the children. The first reading entails teacher support during echo or choral reading. During the second reading, the teacher monitors as the children read with partners or whisper read by themselves.

Each small-group lesson therefore includes a repeated reading of the same segment, an ingredient that is especially effective for struggling students (Chard, Pikulski, & McDonagh, 2006). The lesson combines repeated readings with instructional strategies that systematically reduce teacher support during the second reading. Beginning with a more supportive technique (choral or echo reading) accomplishes three goals: (1) it helps children construct the meaning of the text since their decoding is heavily supported (Stahl, 2008), (2) it assists with the decoding of unfamiliar words, and (3) it models prosodic reading. The lesson concludes with a question or two prompting an inference or summary. Our 15-minute small-group lesson format leads to approximate time allocations shown in Figure 5.2.

Our lesson format is actually a streamlined version of a technique called fluency-oriented reading instruction (FORI; Stahl & Heubach, 2005). In FORI, the same text is read each day in a 5-day cycle. On the first day, the teacher introduces the book and reads it aloud. We believe that these practices, which have been widely recommended (e.g., Moskal & Blachowicz, 2006; Paratore & McCormack, 2005), are acceptable in whole-class settings. In small-group work, however, this a luxury we cannot recommend. Introducing the book is brief and instead of a read-aloud, teacher support is provided in a more participatory way through echo or choral reading. In FORI, the teacher gradu-

1 minute	Teacher introduces a new book or leads the children in summarizing a book in progress, up to the point of today's segment.
5 minutes	Teacher leads a supportive fluency activity (echo or choral reading).
5 minutes	Children engage in a less supportive fluency activity for the same text segment (partner or whisper reading).
4 minutes	Teacher asks inferential questions or prompts a summary.

FIGURE 5.2. Basic structure of a fluency and comprehension lesson.

ally releases responsibility for reading by engaging the children in echo reading on day 2 and choral reading on day 3. Our format compels the teacher to choose between these two techniques, depending on the demands of the text and the children's proficiency. In FORI, day 4 is devoted to partner reading and day 5 to extension activities. Our format likewise proceeds to rereading, but either in pairs (partner reading) or individually (whisper reading). Day 5 of FORI is devoted to extension activities. Since our main focus is fluency, we conclude our 15-minute lesson with only 4 minutes allotted to comprehension development. Kuhn and Woo (2008) have suggested that FORI involves too much repetition of the same text. Instead, they advocate new text segments introduced daily. Our lesson format also adopts this approach. We have endeavored to create a lesson format that preserves the best of both worlds—adequate repetition, gradual release of responsibility to children, and a daily infusion of fresh text.

HOW CAN YOU PLAN THIS INSTRUCTION?

We begin by considering the general characteristics of an effective small-group lesson devoted to fluency and comprehension. Figure 5.3 captures these characteristics in the form of a checklist.

Once a fluency and comprehension group has been formed, the teacher must plan a sequence of lessons around the format outlined earlier in Figure 5.2. Doing so entails the following steps:

Integrated	☐ Screening assessments used with all of the children in a class are used to identify children for this group.
	☐ The targeting of fluency benchmarks reflected in the state curriculum for English language arts connects differentiated instruction to meaningful goals.
Explicit	☐ The targets for this group are fluency and comprehension only; no word recognition is necessary, with the possible exception of some limited work in multisyllabic words.
	☐ The teacher models fluency during each lesson.
	☐ The teacher specifies procedures for all portions of the lesson.
Scaffolded	☐ Fluency activities proceed from more to less teacher support.
	☐ The teacher provides continuing word recognition support during all activities.
Systematic	☐ The teacher has a plan for a series of fluency lessons of similar length and difficulty.
	☐ The teacher has a plan for progress monitoring using established fluency assessment methods.

FIGURE 5.3. Checklist for targeting fluency and comprehension.

1. Select appropriate books.
2. Choose instructional approaches.
3. Formulate comprehension questions.

These steps are relatively straightforward. In fact, of the four basic groups on our differentiation staircase, the fluency and comprehension group is the easiest to plan for.

Which Books Should We Choose?

Unless a book possesses certain features, its effectiveness in building fluency will be limited. It must be written in prose understandable to the children and it must address topics or themes they find interesting. We recommend that the books have a difficulty toward the upper end of the children's grade level. Although not written in patterned or decodable text, the book must nevertheless contain a minimum of challenging multisyllabic words. The length of the book is immaterial, as long as it can be completed in the 3-week cycle. An advantage of longer books is that they present children with the same prose style day after day and with the likelihood that many words will be repeated in later text segments (Chard et al., 2006). We have suggested some guiding questions in checklist form as reminders of these features. These questions appear in Figure 5.4.

Ensuring that the books are comparable in difficulty is not an exact science. Two convenient estimates are the Lexile and the guided reading level. Both estimates may be obtained online at no charge. The Lexile Framework (*www.lexile.com*) provides estimates for a huge database of books, and the Scholastic Reading Counts website (*src. scholastic.com/ecatalog*) provides both Lexile and guided reading levels.

As an example, we located *The Planets*, by Gail Gibbons (2008), in the database and found that this book contains 1,227 words, is written at an approximate readability level of 3.3, corresponds to guided reading level O, may be of interest to children in grades K–2, and has a Lexile score of 660. The Lexile score is a number between 200 and 1,700 that can be translated into an approximate grade range. Although a chart for converting

✓	Guiding Questions
	Is the book written at grade level but toward the upper end of that level?
	Is the book likely to interest the children?
	Does the book contain authentic, natural prose rather than decodable or patterned language?
	Does the text incorporate a limited number of challenging multisyllabic words?
	Can the children complete the book within a 3-week cycle?

FIGURE 5.4. Guidelines for text selection.

Lexile Range	Approximate Readability
200–320	Grade 1
330–360	Grades 1–2
370–420	Grade 2
430–490	Grades 2–3
500–610	Grade 3
620–690	Grades 3–4

FIGURE 5.5. Key Lexile-to-grade-level correspondences for the primary grades.

Lexile scores is available online (*www.lexile.com*), we offer a few useful reference points in Figure 5.5. According to the Lexile system, *The Planets* is slightly more difficult than the estimate provided by Scholastic.

Figure 5.6 displays some familiar authors and titles of books that work well for fluency building in small groups. In addition to the length of the book and the number of chapters, we provide both the Lexile score (and its corresponding grade level) and the guided reading level. These two estimates are in agreement concerning the particular books we have selected. However, this is not always the case. For many books, the two measures produce different estimates of overall difficulty. This is because they rely on different features. The Lexile Framework relies on sentence length and word frequency, but guided reading levels are based on a wider variety of factors, most of which are subjective. These include the length of the book, the size and arrangement of print, the vocabulary represented, the structure of the language used, genre and text structure, predictability and the presence of repeated patterns, and the support provided by illustrations (Fountas & Pinnell, 1996). It is hardly surprising that the two estimates are sometimes at odds.

Remember that estimating readability is not an exact process. Lexile and guided reading levels are merely guidelines for making good choices. Unfortunately, they give us the impression of being more precise than they actually are. Moreover, they do not account for the needs of a particular small group. We urge teachers to exercise their own judgment in cases where established measures produce conflicting results. Teachers will begin each lesson by providing strong assistance, a practice that research suggests is superior to selecting easier books that the children can read initially with only limited help (Kuhn & Stahl, 2003). This fact argues for selecting slightly harder books.

Which Instructional Methods Should We Use?

The lesson format for this group involves three instructional decisions. First, although the main focus will be on repeated readings, some children may benefit from a short warm-up on multisyllabic decoding. We view this activity as a form of fluency instruction because these students can already recognize all the *parts* of these multisyllabic words.

Grade	Words	Chapter	Guided Reading Level	Lexile		Examples
				Score	Grade	
1	105	N/A	H	10L	1	*Whose Mouse Are You?* Robert Kraus (1986)
	281	N/A	I	BR	1	*Albert the Albatross* Syd Hoff (1961)
2	562	N/A	J	350L	1–2	*Henry and Mudge and Mrs. Hopper's House* Cynthia Rylant (2003)
	1,635	N/A	K	380L	2	*Nate the Great and the Missing Key* Marjorie Weinman Sharmat (1982)
	839	N/A	L	400L	2	*Arthur's Teacher Trouble* Marc Brown (1986)
	8,751	10	M	460L	2–3	*Jake Drake, Bully Buster* Andrew Clements (2001)
3	1,150		N	560L	3	*The Man Who Tricked a Ghost* Laurence Yep (1993)
	10,820	13	O	600L	3	*See You Later, Gladiator* Jon Scieszka (2000)
	1,742		P	690L	3–4	*The Ballot Box Battle* Emily Arnold McCully (1996)

FIGURE 5.6. Examples of books corresponding to Lexile and guided reading levels. *Note.* BR, beginning reader, low-level first grade.

They simply need to become faster at applying their skills. For this reason, we believe that many students will benefit from an approach in which teachers include some brief syllable-combining exercises at the beginning of small-group time. However, the teacher must decide whether the needs of a particular group would be best met by this plan.

The second decision involves the initial reading of the text segment. Here, the teacher must choose between echo and choral reading. Both echo and choral reading are highly supportive, but readers whose word recognition skills are not yet firm may derive more benefit from the one–two sequence of echo reading. In choral reading, students must be able to read the text *as* the teacher is reading it. In echo reading, as the teacher reads, students follow along without having to simultaneously apply their skills. Uncertainty about which method to use can be resolved by trial and error. A teacher may discover in the process that both methods work equally well for a given group and a given book, and the two approaches can be varied.

The last decision involves how to approach the second reading of the same segment. The teacher must select between partner or whisper reading. Like echo and choral reading, partner and whisper reading also differ in the amount of support they provide, and the same considerations apply in choosing between them. Students whose word recognition skills are tentative will probably be better served by reading with a partner, but experimenting with a particular group is advisable.

These decisions can be summed up in the following questions:

1. Should the lesson begin with an activity devoted to multisyllabic words?
2. Should the first reading of the text segment be done through echo or choral reading?
3. Should the second reading of the text segment be done through partner or whisper reading?

Each of these decisions requires some planning.

Syllable Types

Discussion of syllable types can be a support to multisyllabic decoding. It is likely to be a part of core instruction, so differentiated lessons can use the same terms that children are accustomed to hearing. This type of support would not be appropriate for first-grade readers; they are not encountering enough multisyllabic words, and they typically have not learned all of the syllable types. Second- and third-grade readers, however, may get bogged down as the words get longer and more complex. The trick is to remind them to use what they know about one-syllable words and apply those skills to longer words. Note that the words are selected for their features rather than simply because they will be encountered in the text. We want children to have skills and strategies for recognizing all words, and syllable types are a useful tool.

We ask the children to decide how to break words into syllables, but teachers need not focus on "correctness" in this area. Rather, any way that an individual child breaks a word into manageable parts is "correct" for that child—if it yields an accurate pronunciation. Decoding practice for this group must be very brief to allow adequate time for our real focus—fluency. For this reason, we create lists of 10 words that could be used in less than 2 minutes.

Echo Reading

For children unfamiliar with echo reading, the teacher must introduce the procedures and lead the group in practicing with very brief amounts of text (Meisinger & Bradley, 2008). Once children are comfortable with the process, the teacher's goal is to decide how much of the text to read each time before pausing for the children to echo it back. There is no research to guide us in this area, but a few sensible conclusions can be offered. For example, breaks should always occur at phrase boundaries, especially those marked by punctuation. These points are where an English speaker would pause, after all, and one goal of echo reading is to model the phrasing of oral language. We recommend reading one or more entire sentences, depending on their length, and rarely pausing within a sentence. In our experience, a common mistake involves reading too little before pausing, out of fear that the students will have difficulties. What happens, though, is that the children do not look at the actual words while the teacher is reading—they simply focus on repeating what the teacher has said. Remember that the goal is to support their rapid word recognition in the context of actual reading. This cannot happen unless the amount of text they must echo exceeds their short-term memory; this forces them to process each word as the teacher first reads it, and then to process it again when it is their turn to read.

Compared with choral reading, during which the teacher's attention is on "performance," echo reading provides a better opportunity to monitor the children. As students read back the text, they should be visually attending to their books and tracking as they read. If students are able to echo a segment without attending to the print, they are relying on memory and the whole point of echo reading is lost. We agree with Rasinski's (2003) suggestion that children finger point as they read so that the teacher can monitor their tracking and so that they must in fact track the print as they echo the text segment. We believe that it is a mistake to try to monitor in more detail. The echo format makes it difficult to tell how individual students are phrasing, for example. Better opportunities arise when they partner or whisper read later in the lesson.

Figure 5.7 summarizes key considerations for conducting echo reading in a small-group format.

Choral Reading

Choral reading is somewhat less supportive than echo reading because children must apply word recognition skills *while* the teacher reads rather than *afterward*. It is an excellent method to use with students who are struggling to become fluent. As Moskal and Blachowicz have observed, these children "are more willing to participate because they hear a fluent rendition and can participate without drawing attention to themselves" (2006, p. 60).

The text segment for a lesson should take about 5 minutes to read at a leisurely pace. Remember that children will be expected to reread the same segment in roughly the same amount of time, either individually or with a partner. There are no stopping points during choral reading. The principal goal is to maximize oral reading practice. In choral reading, it is crucial for the teacher to maintain a natural pace and to model oral inflections in a normal manner. Slight exaggerations for emphasis are permissible because they reinforce the link between prosody and meaning.

---

1. Practice with short segments if students are unfamiliar with the process.
2. Read one or more entire sentences before pausing. (Try not to pause within sentences.)
3. Read enough material that students cannot rely on memory alone.
4. Make sure that children finger point as they read.
5. Monitor to ensure attention to print and tracking.

FIGURE 5.7. Suggestions for echo reading.

As with echo reading, we recommend that children finger point as they read. Observing them as they do so is sufficient monitoring during this phase of the lesson. Remember that you will have a better chance to monitor during the second portion of the lesson.

Many variations of choral reading have been introduced (Rasinski, 2003), such as cumulative choral reading, in which various groups are responsible for assigned text segments. However, these variations are not well suited to small-group work. We recommend establishing a routine in which the teacher always leads the group.

Figure 5.8 summarizes key considerations for conducting choral reading in a small-group format.

Partner Reading

Planning for partner reading entails a number of decisions. The teacher must answer the following questions:

1. Which students should be paired?
2. How should partners be changed over time?
3. How shall the partners sit?
4. How shall the partners read?

Deciding which students to pair is easier in small groups than when partner reading is implemented with an entire class. There is no quandary over whether to pair weaker with stronger readers, for example, because group members are already functioning at similar levels. Rather than permitting children to choose partners, we believe it is better for the teacher to assign them based on seating. Because the group members typically meet at a small table, it is efficient for partner work to occur between children sitting closest to one another. It is in the small-group seating arrangement that the teacher can look ahead to partner reading and seat children next to one another who are likely to work well as a pair. We do not recommend switching partners during a 3-week cycle unless there is evidence that a particular pairing is not working. Allowing children to work with the same partner over an extended period allows them to build a social relationship that is conducive to each partner's learning (Moskal & Blachowicz, 2006).

Deciding where the partners will sit entails a few commonsense considerations. They must be close enough to hear one another in whisper voices. They must be far enough from the others pairs that they are not distracted by them. And they must be

---

1. Keep an eye on the clock and stop after 5 minutes.
2. Do not pause to ask questions or elicit input from children.
3. Make sure that children finger point as they read.
4. Monitor to ensure attention to print and tracking.

FIGURE 5.8. Suggestions for choral reading.

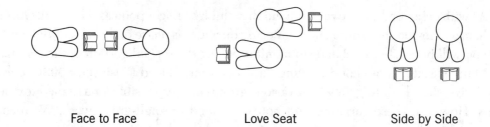

Face to Face   Love Seat   Side by Side

FIGURE 5.9. Three seating arrangements for choral reading.

close enough to the teacher that they can be monitored and, when necessary, supported. We suggest that any of three basic seating arrangements will meet these requirements. These are represented in Figure 5.9. There is no research to help us choose among them, and we encourage teachers to experiment and to consider deliberately varying the arrangement.

Deciding how the partners will read is also simplified by the homogeneous nature of the small group. It is important, first, that we clarify the term *partner reading*. Because the partners are functioning at nearly the same level, this activity is similar to *buddy reading* (Rasinski, 2003). It differs from buddy reading, however, in that students are closely monitored and do not choose their own books. Partner reading is really a form of *paired reading*, but in most types of paired reading one partner is considerably more proficient than the other (Meisinger & Bradley, 2008). All this may sound confusing. The important thing is that partner reading in small, differentiated groups involves two children at comparable levels of fluency. With respect to how they read, we recommend that they take turns. The teacher must establish a rule as to how long a turn should last (e.g., a page or a paragraph). As one student reads, the other listens and lends support with word recognition if need be. The partners do not discuss the content or ask each other questions. That will come later. Partnering provides a second chance to practice oral reading for a full 5 minutes.

Figure 5.10 summarizes key considerations for conducting partner reading in a small-group format.

Whisper Reading

The least supportive fluency activity is whisper reading. Remember, however, that support has already been provided in the form of echo or choral reading. Whisper reading involves the second exposure to a text segment that has been highly supported at a previous point in the lesson. Despite this support, however, the teacher must judge whether partner reading would be a more effective alternative to whisper reading. This judgment should be made on the basis of the students' proficiency and the particular demands of the text. Some experimenting may be needed to make the best choice for a particular book.

During whisper reading, children read simultaneously but, unlike choral reading, they do not read in unison. We describe their reading as asynchronous. It is important for

1. Assign partners based on compatibility.
2. Do not change partners during the 3-week cycle.
3. Seat children so that they are next to their partners at the beginning of the lesson.
4. Use any of the three basic seating arrangements for partner work.
5. Make sure that children understand the procedure, which includes these rules:
   - Take turns.
   - Listen and follow along in the book while your partner reads.
   - Be polite if you help your partner.
   - Follow the (teacher-made) rule about how much to read.
   - Don't talk about other things.
   - Tell the teacher if there are problems.
6. Monitor each pair, offering help as needed.

FIGURE 5.10. Suggestions for partner reading.

teachers to make clear to the children that they are not to read chorally and that in fact they should ignore the other group members. It may be useful to spread the children out a bit or to use whisper phones to help minimize noise pollution.

As the children whisper read, the teacher is in a position to monitor. The situation may seem a little cacophonous at first because all of the children are reading at the same time but at slightly different points in the text. The teacher may not know which way to turn! The solution is to be systematic. Listen to one child for awhile, then another, and so on, always being mindful of the need to assist with word recognition. It is a good idea to make a rule that a child in need of help with a word will silently signal the teacher. One way is to have the child hold the book toward the teacher with a finger under the word.

Figure 5.11 summarizes key considerations for conducting whisper reading in a small-group format.

Which Questions Should We Ask?

The final portion of the lesson is devoted to comprehension questions that prompt the children to make connections between facts they have read and facts they knew in advance. These inferential questions are sometimes speculative but more often have fac-

1. Make a rule about how to ask for help.
2. Be sensitive to the possibility that whisper reading may be too hard, and be ready to use partner reading instead.
3. Remind students to attend only to their own voices.
4. Remind students to use whisper voices.
5. Monitor one child at a time.
6. Provide pronunciations as needed.

FIGURE 5.11. Suggestions for whisper reading.

tual answers not explicitly stated in the text. Such questions can involve making predictions, inferring cause-and-effect relationships, inferring unspecified details, or arriving at main ideas, to name a few. The nature of a text segment should determine the questions asked. Not all types of questions are relevant to a given selection.

Figure 5.12 provides examples of inferential questions based on *Little Red Riding Hood*. Note that although the children can answer them, the answers cannot be found in the story. Questions like these are excellent for prompting a deeper understanding of text and also for preparing children for the questions that will confront them on high-stakes achievement tests (McKenna & Stahl, 2009).

STRATEGIES FOR EVERY PUPIL RESPONSE

The beauty of these lessons is that every pupil response is a built-in feature of the fluency activities. Each type of reading—echo, choral, partner, and whisper—requires students to be actively engaged at all times. At no time are individual children singled out while others tread water waiting their turn. In the case of the inferential questioning, creative teachers can also find ways to engage all of the children. For example, in asking for a prediction about what will happen in the next segment, the teacher might ask the children to share a prediction with their partner.

TAKING STOCK

At the conclusion of a 3-week lesson cycle, the teacher conducts an assessment to determine whether the children should remain in the fluency and comprehension group or advance to vocabulary and comprehension. This assessment involves asking each child to read a new sample of grade-level text, recording the words read correctly in 1 minute, and comparing the score with established benchmarks for the beginning, middle, or end of the year.

Figure 5.13 shows how one set of benchmarks, those used in the DIBELS battery, rise during each year. (The fact that they appear to fall slightly at the beginning of second

Skill	Sample Question
Prediction	What do you think would have happened if the hunter hadn't arrived?
Cause and Effect	Why did the wolf pretend to be Little Red Riding Hood's grandmother?
Detail	Why do you think the wolf didn't eat Little Red Riding Hood when he met her in the woods?
Main Idea	How could we tell this story in just a few sentences?

FIGURE 5.12. Inferential questions based on *Little Red Riding Hood*.

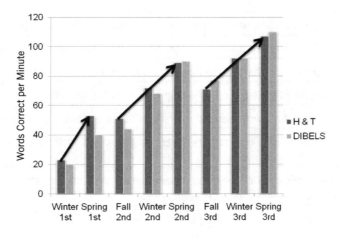

FIGURE 5.13. Benchmarks for Oral Reading Fluency from DIBELS and from Hasbrouck and Tindal (2006).

and third grades is because the readability of the materials is calibrated near the end of these grades.) The upward arrows show the target trajectory for each grade. A child who attains the benchmark at one point in time will qualify for the highest group (vocabulary and comprehension).

The passages used for the assessment can be downloaded (at no charge) from the DIBELS website (*www.dibels.uoregon.edu*), but curriculum-based fluency assessment, which might involve passages that accompany a core program, can also be used. The DIBELS approach requires that three independent samples be taken and that only the middle score be compared with the benchmark. Given the variations that occur among texts, this is probably a wise policy for curriculum-based assessment as well. With a group of four children there will be enough time for this process. For a larger group, more time will be needed, but it might be concluded later in the day. It is important to note that the benchmarks for DIBELS refer only to the DIBELS passages themselves. These passages are read "cold" with no support from teacher or pictures. For first-grade readers especially, this means that the benchmarks must reflect the difficulty of that kind of task. A widely cited set of benchmarks for children reading in natural texts (Hasbrouck & Tindal, 2006) targets higher reading rates for children performing at the 50th percentile. Figure 5.13 also provides a comparison of these two sets of benchmarks. We recommend that teachers attend to these higher goals when children are reading actual books. Note that neither set of benchmarks target fall of first grade, when children are typically building their word recognition skills.

Finally, we assess only fluency for this group even though comprehension was a second focus. There are two reasons for this policy. The first is that general comprehension proficiency cannot be measured reliably in a brief time. The second is that even if the teacher decides to advance a child to a higher group, comprehension will still be one of the targets.

Step 1	Use student performance data to formulate (or reformulate) all groups.
Step 2	Select books for the entire cycle based on comparable difficulty and interest.
Step 3	Choose one book from the set you have selected for a 3-week cycle.
Step 4	Determine segments for each day's lesson based on the time they are likely to require.
Step 5	For each text segment, write several inferential comprehension questions.
Step 6	Based on the proficiency of group members, decide whether to take 1 or 2 minutes to practice multisyllabic decoding.
Step 7	Based on the proficiency of group members, decide whether the initial reading of the segment should involve echo or choral reading.
Step 8	Decide whether the second reading of the segment should involve partner or whisper reading.

FIGURE 5.14. Overall steps in planning a fluency and comprehension lesson.

SUMMARY

The fluency and comprehension lessons we have described contain the most effective features that research has identified. You will see our lessons in Appendix 5.1. The lessons include brief daily practice, repeated oral reading of passages, consistency in text style and vocabulary, teacher modeling, corrective feedback, partner reading, and assessment geared to fluency benchmarks (Chard et al., 2006). The lesson format we have described incorporates these features systematically. The steps in planning a lesson using this format are outlined in Figure 5.14. Steps 3–7 are repeated for each book in the set.

LESSON PLANS

Planning for this group is simple, but we still provide tools for a teacher to use to get the hang of this instruction. We have chosen three potential achievement profiles—a first-grade group, a second-grade group, and a third-grade group—and we have selected texts from the end of each of those grade levels. Plans like these can be made quickly and used immediately. The most important consideration is how to write questions that really tap inferential thinking. We think that just one set of our lesson plans will be enough for a teacher to become proficient with this task for this group.

We also provide three sets of advanced decoding lessons. Each is a word list, targeting a particular combination of syllable types. There are six major syllable types. In closed syllables (e.g., *trash*) the vowel is short and followed by one or more consonants. In open syllables (e.g., *re*mote) the vowel comes at the end of the syllable and is pronounced with its long sound. Vowel teams include any two vowels (and sometimes *w* or *y*) working together to represent one sound (e.g., con*tain*). Consonant–*l*–*e* syllables always come at the end of words (e.g., ena*ble*). Vowel–consonant–*e* syllables come at the end of words or are affected by the dropped *e* when suffixes are added (e.g., en*rage*, *blam*ing). R-controlled syllables link a vowel and *r* in the production of one sound (e.g., sh*ark*).

Multisyllabic Decoding Practice

Let's warm up with some word reading. Remember that you know everything you need to know to read long words. When you see a new word, look for the vowel patterns, decode each syllable, and then blend and check. The words I have today have one consonant–*l*–*e* syllable. Remember that final *e* does not signal a long vowel; isolate those last three letters and pronounce the syllable that is left. You'll have to decide whether it is open or closed. And then blend the two syllables. When you're done, we'll do them together.

Day 1	Day 2	Day 3	Day 4	Day 5
apple	bottle	wiggle	bubble	bundle
chuckle	fumble	bugle	able	amble
jungle	knuckle	mumble	cradle	gamble
ankle	bridle	cackle	candle	castle
cable	cripple	cuddle	cycle	dimple
fable	fiddle	freckle	gentle	giggle
grumble	handle	hustle	idle	juggle
mantle	maple	middle	nestle	noble
paddle	pebble	pickle	puzzle	riddle
saddle	single	title	triple	twinkle
waffle	whistle	wrinkle	drizzle	settle

(continued)

Multisyllabic Decoding Practice *(page 2 of 3)*

Let's warm up with some word reading. Remember that you know everything you need to know to read long words. When you see a new word, look for the vowel patterns, decode each syllable, and then blend and check. The words I have today have one open syllable. That means that the vowel is at the end and it is long. And they might have a vowel–consonant–*e* syllable; you know that means that the vowel is also long, or an *r*-controlled syllable representing the sound in *car, for,* or *purr*. Draw a line where you think the syllables are, and then read the word. When you're done, we'll do them together.

Day 1	Day 2	Day 3	Day 4	Day 5
crater	labor	radar	savor	vapor
cedar	female	femur	fever	meter
cider	spider	miser	tiger	visor
donate	gopher	locate	motor	odor
rotate	lemur	humor	rumor	tutor
paper	super	clover	rebate	remote
refute	acorn	polite	decide	require
erase	device	recline	recite	revive
provide	supreme	delete	deceive	precise
oblige	decode	propose	promote	dilute
fiber	grocer	mobile	rebate	rebuke

(continued)

Let's warm up with some word reading. Remember that you know everything you need to know to read long words. When you see a new word, look for the vowel patterns, decode each syllable, and then blend and check. I'm going to give you a list of words. Each word has one syllable with a vowel team. You'll have to be flexible about that vowel sound. There is also one closed syllable. It will represent the short sound or the schwa. Draw a line where you think the syllables are, and then read the word. When you're done, we'll do them together.

Day 1	Day 2	Day 3	Day 4	Day 5
afraid	await	campaign	complain	contain
exclaim	explain	mailbox	mainland	raisin
sustain	dismay	grayish	payment	ahead
breakfast	deafen	heaven	instead	meadow
pheasant	pleasant	steadfast	treadmill	weapon
asleep	canteen	exceed	greenish	increase
mislead	reason	peanut	caffeine	lightning
roadblock	approach	disown	sheerest	deerskin
fearful	gearshift	annoy	cashew	baboon
trowel	employ	tighten	spearmint	teardrop

Sample Lessons for a First-Grade Group

Henry and Mudge, by Cynthia Rylant (1996)

All lessons take the same format.	

1. What do we already know about these characters? or Let's review what we learned in yesterday's reading.
2. Choral or echo read.
3. Partner or whisper read. See whether you can improve your expression.
4. Discussion.

Reading	Questions for Discussion
The First Book pp. 5–22	Why do you think Henry didn't want a dog with curly hair? Why did Henry stop worrying after he got Mudge? Why did Mudge love Henry's bed?
The First Book pp. 23–end	How did Henry know that Mudge must be lost? How did Mudge find Henry? What did Henry and Mudge dream about?
Puddle Trouble: The Snow Glory	Why didn't Henry's mother want him to pick the snow glory? Why did Henry want to pick it? Why did Henry call Mudge a bad dog?
Puddle Trouble: Puddle Trouble	Why did Henry call one of the puddles an "ocean puddle"? Why wasn't Henry's father angry at him?
Puddle Trouble: The Kittens	What was the new dog going to do? How did Mudge stop him? Why do you think Mudge lay down beside the box?
Green Time: The Picnic	What did Mudge have for dessert? Which food did Henry and Mudge share? How did Mudge get Henry to stop crying?
Green Time: The Bath	How did Mudge know he was going to get a bath? Which part of the bath did Mudge hate the most? How did Mudge get Henry back?
Green Time: The Green Time	Why did Henry feel big? Do you think Mudge really ate monsters? Why not?
Under the Yellow Moon: Together in the Fall	Why were none of the leaves green? Who can tell me one way that Henry and Mudge did things differently? What does the author mean by saying, "Henry put on a coat and Mudge grew one"?
Under the Yellow Moon: Under the Yellow Moon	Why do you think Henry's mother dressed up before telling stories? Why do you think Henry's mother told ghost stories if she knew the stories scared Henry? Why did Henry think the clicking sound might be shoes?
Under the Yellow Moon: Thanksgiving Guest	How many weeks did Aunt Sally stay at Henry's house? Why did Henry think Aunt Sally would hate Mudge? What made Henry like Aunt Sally?
Sparkle Days: Sparkle Days	Why did Henry call it a "sparkle day"? Why did Mudge bark at Henry? Why didn't Mudge get mad when Henry threw a snowball at him?
Sparkle Days: Firelight	Why did Henry and his parents like to take walks even though it was cold? Why do you think Mudge wagged his tail? What made the wood pop?

Sample Lessons for a Second-Grade Group

Cam Jansen and the Chocolate Fudge Mystery, by David Adler (1993)

All lessons take the same format.
1. What do we already know about these characters? or Let's review what we learned in yesterday's reading.
2. Choral or echo read the next chapter.
3. Partner or whisper read that same chapter. See whether you can improve your expression.
4. Discussion.

Reading	Questions for Discussion
Chapter 1	Why is Cam a good nickname for Jennifer Jansen? Why was Cam suspicious of the woman, but not the runners? What do you think the woman may be hiding?
Chapter 2	What is odd about the fact that the woman puts her trash in the trash can? Why do you think Eric is uneasy? What do you think is in the bag?
Chapter 3	How do you think Cam felt after looking in the trash? How do you think Eric felt? Why did the kids think no one was home? Who do you think is chasing the kids?
Chapter 4	Who was actually chasing the kids? Why? Why does Eric think no one is home? Why does Cam disagree? Who do you think is right?
Chapter 5	Why does Cam's father ask the Millers' permission for Cam to stay in their yard? Why does Mrs. Miller think that the nephew might be in the house? Why are the newspapers a clue for Cam?
Chapter 6	Why is the newspaper headline an important clue? How would it help Cam to know when the man went into hiding? Why does Mrs. Miller still think it's the Pells' nephew? How do the dates on the newspapers help Cam to identify the man?
Chapter 7	Why is Mr. Jansen unable to speak clearly to the policeman? What do you think the woman was going to do with the suitcase? Why did the woman leave her disguise in the store?
Chapter 8	How did Cam know what clothing the woman had on under her raincoat? Why do you think the woman admitted that she was involved with the bank robber? How does the captain decide to thank Cam and Eric for their help? How does Cam impress the police officers?

Sample Lessons for a Third-Grade Group

See You Later, Gladiator, by Jon Scieszka (2000)

All lessons take the same format. 1. What do we already know about these characters? or Let's review what we learned in yesterday's reading. 2. Choral or echo read the next chapter. 3. Partner or whisper read that same chapter. See whether you can improve your expression. 4. Discussion.	

Reading	Questions for Discussion
Chapter 1	What is a gladiator? What do you think gladiators do? What does Sam mean when he says, "And maybe I'm Santa Claus and maybe this is the North Pole"? Why do the kids need to find *The Book*? What kind of book do you think it is? What do you think will happen next?
Chapter 2	Why does the author tell us the history of *The Book*? How does *The Book* work? Why did the Time Warp Trio get stuck in the world of the gladiator?
Chapter 3	How can we tell that the gladiator would not really have harmed the boys? Why did Dorkius have a hard time telling when the boys would graduate?
Chapter 4	How did the boys plan to find out where the library was? Why did the boys use such bad manners while they ate? What do you think the boys will do when they finish eating?
Chapter 5	Why were the boys confused about the word *circus*? Did all gladiators fight other gladiators? Why did the Professor want to become a Roman citizen?
Chapter 6	How did Joe keep the gladiators from hitting the plate with the trident? What does it mean, in Judo, never to meet a force head on? What do you think Brutus will do now that Joe beat him?
Chapter 7	Why do you think Sam decided to throw grapes at the gladiators? Why did the Professor decide to help the boys find the book? What do you think Dorkius will do now that he's found the boys?
Chapter 8	Why did the Professor admire the Romans even though they had made him a slave? What did the men use instead of soap? Is Joe really about to be killed by a gladiator? What do you think will happen?
Chapter 9	How did Joe escape being killed? Did it surprise you? What is a vomitorium for? What do you think will happen when the boys fight the Professor?
Chapter 10	Why did the blindfold plan work so well? Why did earning their citizenship not get the boys out of trouble? What do you think will happen when Brutus and Horridus catch them?
Chapter 11	Why could the boys understand people when they spoke but could not read signs? Why was the bookstore closed? Do you think the boys will really be buried alive? Why or why not?
Chapter 12	Why do you think the woman helped the boys? Do you think there were books in Rome, or just scrolls? What do think happened to the Professor?
Chapter 13	How did the boys know the Professor was all right? Do you think Brutus and Horridus were really turned into statues?

Chapter 6

TARGETING VOCABULARY AND COMPREHENSION

The chance for teachers to truly target vocabulary and comprehension development during precious small-group time is the reward for implementing and evaluating the effects of instruction in lower-level skills. Children in this group have reached the highest step on our staircase. In kindergarten and first grade, these children are making excellent progress in acquiring decoding skills. In grades 2 and 3, they have also attained grade-level fluency. Figure 6.1 shows which children qualify for this group. Unlike the groups on the lower steps, there is no exit ticket for these children. Our goal is to keep them at this level indefinitely. There is always the possibility of their moving *downward*, perhaps needing a temporary return to fluency work. That is why periodic assessment is still required.

Grade Levels	Characteristics of Children	Small-Group Instructional Approach
K–1	Children have achieved benchmark levels in phonological awareness and word recognition. They typically are *not* fluent readers but are acquiring word recognition skills at an appropriate pace.	Children are exposed through read-alouds to texts that are challenging but comprehensible.
2–3	Children are fluent readers. They have acquired word recognition skills and can apply them rapidly while reading grade-level text.	Children read grade-level texts, with teacher support, for developing vocabulary and applying comprehension strategies.

FIGURE 6.1. Children whose needs are best met through vocabulary and comprehension.

Instruction for this group always centers around a trade book. In a 3-week cycle, from 3 to 15 books might be used, depending on their length and complexity. The books teachers choose can vary in genre and text organization but should be at roughly the same level of difficulty. Their content may be tied to standards in English language arts, science, and social studies, but the chief reading goal at this level is to provide the children with a variety of engaging text types, rich with vocabulary and ripe with opportunities to apply comprehension strategies.

WHO NEEDS THIS INSTRUCTION?

Differentiated instruction for these readers is not remedial in nature. There is in fact nothing to remediate. For this reason, it is easy to ignore these children, to assume that they will naturally advance with little guidance on the part of teachers, and so teachers often provide them with no explicit instruction in small-group settings. After all, are there not many children in our classrooms who need instruction more? We beg to differ with this stance. We believe that all children deserve focused attention on their needs as developing readers, and we therefore plan small-group instruction with the goal of extending their vocabulary knowledge and their ability to comprehend increasingly complex text. Truly differentiated reading instruction serves all children.

Because this level is the most advanced, it is tempting to assume that all of these children are fluent readers who merely need to expand their vocabulary and enhance their comprehension proficiency. In the case of second and third graders, this assumption is correct. But what about beginners, who are acquiring decoding skills at a rate consistent with the grade-level curriculum and state standards? What is the best course to take with these children in small-group work? We do not believe it makes sense to provide additional decoding-focused instruction during small-group time since they have learned all that we have endeavored to teach and we have reason to believe that they will continue to do so. Such a focus would not constitute differentiation at all. To sum up, these lessons are intended for two types of children: those in kindergarten or first grade who, although they are making good progress, are not yet fluent; and those in second or third grade who have achieved fluency.

The case for targeting vocabulary and comprehension for these children is simple and compelling. In Chapter 2, we noted that the cognitive model of reading assessment implies that students must have adequate vocabulary and comprehension proficiency if they are to read and understand grade-level text. Children must be familiar with an increasing number of word meanings if they are to extract meaning from more and more demanding texts. At they same time, they must also be able to apply a variety of familiar comprehension strategies to unfamiliar texts. The National Assessment of Educational Progress (NAEP; 2007) has documented that 33% of fourth graders were reading below a basic level by fourth-grade standards. Perhaps many of these children will be identified and served in word recognition and fluency groups or in fluency and comprehension groups. However, NAEP data also reveal that only 33% of the nation's fourth graders can be considered proficient and a mere 8% are reading at an advanced level. This is a cumulative problem that has its roots in the earlier grades. Biemiller (2004) has pointed out that nothing systematic is done to help children learn the word meanings they will need if they are to comprehend the texts they will encounter in the upper grades. Observational studies of comprehension instruction (e.g., Durkin, 1978) make the same case for the paucity of comprehension instruction during elementary school.

In the case of beginning readers, there was a time when authorities advised caution in promoting vocabulary and comprehension instruction before children attained fluency. Teachers were advised to wait until children had attained fluency and until the end of the "developmental shift" that typically occurs between the ages of 5 and 7. This shift is characterized by children's ability to think in multidimensional terms about what they read, which is important if they are to apply comprehension strategies (Smolkin & Donovan, 2002). Only then, it was argued, can children take full advantage of comprehension instruction (Paris, Searnio, & Cross, 1986). Reading researchers have now abandoned this view, realizing that read-alouds can be instrumental in building vocabulary and strategic comprehension long before decoding enables children to apply these skills on their own (Smolkin & Donovan, 2002).

In the case of older readers who have attained adequate fluency to read grade-level material with adequate speed and expression, there was a time when many teachers regarded these students as accomplished readers, requiring only the routine exposure to basal stories and perhaps time spent reading on their own. This view constitutes wishful thinking. We do not deny the importance of fluency, but it would be a mistake to view it as the chief goal of reading instruction in the primary grades. Fluency is necessary but not sufficient for adequate comprehension. We cannot afford to ignore the developmental needs of children who are fluent in order to address the needs of those who are not. In our system of differentiated instruction, the needs of both types of readers can be addressed. A painful "either/or" choice is unnecessary.

WHAT DOES THIS INSTRUCTION LOOK LIKE?

For the decoding-focused groups (the first two steps on our staircase), we propose a series of small groups, each slightly more advanced than the one before. For the top step, at which vocabulary and comprehension are the targets, this kind of progression takes a different form. Our goal is to vary the text type (narrative and various expository structures) while gradually selecting more advanced texts. Our path is not a straight line but a spiral. Figure 6.2 illustrates how we slowly move from easier to harder texts, at the same time varying their structure. Perhaps at this level the image of a spiral staircase works best.

Does it matter what kinds of books we select for these groups, as long as the material provides an appropriate level of challenge? A major consideration is whether to use narrative or expository books. Our own experiences with reading novels versus textbooks might prompt us to begin with narrative materials and progress to information text. There is indeed some evidence that narrative text is easier to comprehend than expository, when readability factors are comparable (see Leslie & Caldwell, 2005). However, there is a

Harder Texts

Easier Texts

Rotation among Major Text Types

FIGURE 6.2. A spiral plan for vocabulary and comprehension.

hidden trap in this kind of thinking: If we begin exclusively with narrative literature, we run the risk of never transitioning to information text. Duke (2000) has documented the startling rarity of nonfiction books in the primary grades. In addition, the longstanding myth that children prefer fiction has been put to rest (Duke & Bennett-Armistead, 2003). (We suspect it may actually be primary *teachers* who prefer fiction.) Given the central role played by information text in the upper elementary years and beyond, it would be foolish to wait. And considering the range of organizational patterns used by the authors of information texts, it is important to expose young children to a variety of text types and genres so that they can develop a knowledge of the unique demands of each (Duke & Bennett-Armistead, 2003).

Were we to visit a classroom during small-group time, we would expect to observe certain elements in a lesson conducted with children at this level. Instruction would center around a specific trade book, either fiction or nonfiction. The teacher would have selected a small number of words, either general or technical, on which to focus. The teacher would also have selected one or two comprehension strategies to review in the context of the book. Research-based methods would be employed to teach these words and strategies, and the teacher would ensure active engagement by using every pupil response techniques and by maintaining a brisk instructional pace. Accomplishing all of this is simpler than it may sound. In the following sections, we offer specific suggestions for making it all happen.

HOW CAN YOU PLAN THIS INSTRUCTION?

Because every small-group lesson at this level centers around a trade book, the first order of business is to select a book. This is really a three-step process. The first step is to decide on a specific focus for 3 weeks of work. In our model lessons, you will see that we have chosen one thematic unit about sea mammals and one author study for a set of narratives by William Steig. The next step is to choose related books for the entire 3-week cycle that vary in some ways but are similar in difficulty. The third step is to sequence these books in order to provide a logical progression as well as some variety in type and length. We believe that it is best to have a combination of shorter and longer books, perhaps using the shortest book first. Short books contain a few new words and can be read in one small-group session. Longer books may contain many new words and can be read in parts, over several days.

✓	Guiding Questions
	Does the text connect to other texts or other parts of the curriculum?
	Is the text likely to be comprehensible given teacher support?
	Does the text avoid decodable and patterned language?
	Does the text have adequate content to foster comprehension development?
	Does the text incorporate a limited number of important, unfamiliar words?
	Does the content relate to state standards for the English language arts, social studies, or science?
	How many days would it take to finish?

FIGURE 6.3. Guidelines for text selection.

In selecting each book for a 3-week set, it is useful to ask a few key questions about its characteristics. These questions appear in Figure 6.3. Assessing difficulty (to ensure that texts chosen for 3 weeks are fairly comparable and at an appropriate level of difficulty) is extremely important. Even for kindergarten and first grade, where the teacher will read them aloud, the books need to be comprehensible. Their language and content must be within the grasp of these young learners. We recommend that teacher judgment be complemented by a quick reference to online databases such as the Scholastic Reading Counts website (*src.scholastic.com/ecatalog/default.asp*) mentioned in Chapter 5. It provides at no cost the guided reading level, word count, a readability estimate, and the approximate interest level. As with all measures of text difficulty, however, it is important to view these scores as estimates only. They can nevertheless be useful in selecting and sequencing books for a 3-week cycle.

Once a specific book has been selected, instructional planning centers around two broad questions: what to teach and how to teach it. Because each book is unique, there are no uniform answers to these questions. Teachers must use informed insights to size up the book and make instructional decisions that are likely to ensure that the lesson will accomplish its goals.

Which Words and Strategies Should We Teach?

Unlike decoding, vocabulary and comprehension are two areas that cannot be easily broken down into component parts. We have no developmental theories that would help us describe a child as functioning at this stage or that. As we noted in Chapter 2, there are no diagnostic tests of vocabulary or comprehension to help us identify the skills and strategies on which we need to focus. Where does this leave us in planning small-group instruction for these children? Actually, the situations we face in planning vocabulary and comprehension instruction are surprisingly different. Let's examine each one in turn.

In planning for vocabulary, we must choose from a huge number of words. (The editors of the *Oxford English Dictionary* suggest that English contains more words than any other language. See *www.oed.com*.) The choices become more manageable by separating words into two categories. In the case of nonfiction text, we teach technical terms associated with a particular subject area. Because these terms are nested within a particular book, it is the choice of *book* that matters. A particular book about flowers will guide teachers to attend to words like *petal, pistil,* and *stamen*; a book about government might prompt them to explain such words as *legislature* and *bill*. Selecting books based on science and social studies standards makes sense as small-group instruction can be dovetailed with activities in these subjects.

The case of fiction is different. The author's purpose does not include presenting new concepts associated with a content subject. For fiction, we choose what Beck, McKeown, and Kucan (2002) call Tier 2 words, those that are important for academic success, are not associated with a particular content area, and are unlikely to be acquired through conversation. This approach is in direct contrast to the one that we once assumed was the best—to teach directly the most obscure words in every text. The problem with that approach is that those words might be so rare that students will not see them again or have a chance to use them. More useful words include words like *unfortunate* and *apologize*. Although there is no comprehensive list of Tier 2 words, this definition makes it fairly easy to identify them. Our goal in differentiated reading instruction is not to "cover" all Tier 2 words (an impossible task), nor are we concerned about pretesting children's knowledge of the ones we select. We needn't worry about whether the vocabulary words are more familiar to some children than others, because on average at least 12 exposures to a word in various contexts are needed to gain adequate knowledge of its meaning (Stahl & Nagy, 2005). That fact might help, if you turn it into a guiding question: Which words in this book are not totally familiar to my students, but are likely, if presented well, to be used or encountered often enough to really build firm understanding?

In planning for comprehension, we must choose from a limited number of key strategies that proficient readers employ. Such strategies include predicting, monitoring understanding, self-questioning, visualizing, inferring, using fix-up strategies, discerning main ideas, retelling, and synthesizing. This is the opposite problem we face with vocabulary. At first, it may be tempting to view this goal as easily attainable. All we need to do is list the strategies and teach each of them to mastery. If only it were that simple! The catch is that, as they mature as readers, children need to be able to apply the strategies to texts that are increasingly sophisticated. They must be able to discern which strategies are appropriate to a given text and apply them in flexible combinations. These are metacognitive proficiencies that result from varied experiences with texts over long periods of time. Euclid, the Greek mathematician, was once asked by his king if there weren't some shortcut by which a busy ruler might learn geometry. "There is no royal road to geometry," Euclid replied. Likewise there is no quick path to comprehension strategy instruction— no fast track (Block & Paris, 2008). Readers must follow different roads to arrive at the same destination, but some children will need more "directions" than others.

As with vocabulary, teachers must consider the book in deciding which strategies to target during small-group lessons. The good news is that there is a small set of strate-

Vocabulary	For fiction, choose from two to four Tier 2 words, even though their meanings are unrelated.
	For information text, choose the key technical terms introduced by the author. These terms are naturally related in "clusters."
Comprehension	For fiction, focus on story elements. There will also be opportunities to foster children's ability to predict, to monitor their understanding, to self-question, to visualize, to make inferences, to use fix-up strategies, to discern main ideas, to retell, and to synthesize.
	For information text, size up the book, considering how it is organized. Use text structure as a focus. As in the case of fiction, there will also be opportunities to foster inferring, summarizing, and other strategies that apply to all reading.

FIGURE 6.4. Guidelines for deciding what to teach.

gies, and individuals never really master them—so teachers need not fear repeating the strategic focus. In fact, that is the goal. Teachers can take strategies initially introduced in grade-level instruction and guide children to apply them to different texts and text types. It is also why we do not "pretest" or "posttest" them. It is best to select one or two strategies for a particular text and to focus on others as new texts are introduced. We don't worry about whether the children seem proficient in a particular comprehension strategy. What is important is that they have repeated opportunities to apply the strategies in new contexts.

To sum up, once a book has been selected, addressing the two questions in Figure 6.4 is the next order of business.

Which Instructional Methods Should We Use?

We find it useful to divide this question into two parts. The first part involves general features of effective small-group instruction. These features are listed in Figure 6.5, which we are using as a recurrent checklist for planning and observing. The second part is more specific. It entails the instructional approaches that are likely to be most effective in teaching a *particular* set of words and a *particular* set of comprehension strategies in a *particular* trade book. To help you select these approaches, we draw on those methods of instruction with rich histories of research. They are easy to apply, and unlike the decoding-focused small groups the materials you will need are limited.

For vocabulary, we suggest employing one of the well-researched methods listed in Figure 6.6. You will notice that there are fewer approaches for teaching unrelated general words than for a cluster of technical terms. Figure 6.6 provides a quick description of each approach. For a more thorough overview, you can refer to *Differentiated Reading Instruction* (Walpole & McKenna, 2007), or we invite you to examine the lesson plans in Appendix 6.1. These plans provide examples of how the techniques are implemented.

For comprehension, we recommend *explaining* the selected strategy (Duffy's term, 2009) by modeling its use and prompting students to use it. Figure 6.7 lists key com-

Integrated	☐ Comprehension strategies and graphic organizers used in grade-level instruction and then applied to new texts make instruction for this group coherent with the rest of their day.
	☐ The targeting of concepts in the state curriculum for English language arts, science, and social studies connects differentiated instruction to meaningful goals.
Explicit	☐ The targets for this group are only vocabulary and comprehension; there is no fluency building necessary.
	☐ The teacher names the focus skill or strategy.
	☐ The teacher models the focus skill or strategy.
Scaffolded	☐ Group size facilitates attention and practice.
	☐ The teacher provides extended guided practice, with every student responding, through discussion and through writing.
Systematic	☐ The teacher has a plan for a series of lessons for the group.
	☐ The teacher has a plan for progress monitoring.

FIGURE 6.5. Checklist for targeting vocabulary and comprehension.

prehension strategies together with suggestions for how you might explain them. Note that this chart is organized differently than Figure 6.6 for vocabulary. The left-hand column of Figure 6.6 is the instructional technique, not the content, which is of course the actual words to be taught. In Figure 6.7, the left-hand column *is* the content to be taught because a full listing of the key strategies used by proficient readers is possible. The instructional technique that might be used by the teacher is captured in the second and third columns.

It is also important to discuss with children how the text is structured. In introducing the book, the teacher should indicate how the author has organized the prose. There is a limited number of basic text structures, and an author nearly always chooses from among these, sometimes in their simple form and sometimes in combination (McKenna & Robinson, 2009). Figure 6.8 contains the major text structures in common use. A quick review of them will make clear that the more complex structures are encountered principally in nonfiction. This is one reason for making sure that the book selections for this group are balanced to include many titles from science and social studies. It is important to expose children to a wide variety of text structures.

Our experience is that, with the exception of sequential organization used in fiction, these text structures are rarely found in their "pure" form. A combination of the basic types is the rule rather than the exception. For example, the author of a trade book that describes sources of energy may use simple listing to present the sources, but follow these with a section that compares and contrasts them. A book on the problem of the disappearing rain forest may use simple listing to present possible solutions, at the same

Instructional Technique	Information Book	Fiction	Description of Technique
Concept of Definition	✓	✓	The word to be taught is the center of a web. An upward line connects the word to a larger concept; downward lines to smaller concepts. Lateral lines connect to characteristics, and so on. This diagram is constructed with explanation from the teacher. This approach works best with nouns, either general or technical. (An example of this technique can be found in the Sea Mammals Unit, Lesson 1.)
Semantic Feature Analysis	✓		A chart places the name of a category in the upper left-hand box, with category members below. Features the members may or may not possess are written in the top row and the remainder of the chart is filled in with plusses and minuses. The teacher leads the students in comparing and contrasting category members or features. (An example of this technique can be found in the Sea Mammals Unit, Lesson 14.)
Semantic Maps	✓		Like concept of definition, the word to be taught is the center of a web. The word represents the major topic of the book. Lines connect the word to subtopics and information about each, written in brief. Semantic maps are useful for text structure as well but are also key to helping students organize their knowledge of an important concept.
Diagrams	✓		Diagrams are graphic organizers that display how key concepts are related. Principal types include labeled pictures, hierarchical (tree) diagrams, Venns, time lines, and scales. Research shows that they are most effective when they are fully explained by the teacher and when students are given a chance to contribute.
Concept Sort	✓		Key words are presented to students, who work individually, with a partner, or in teams to categorize them. In a closed sort, the teacher supplies the category labels. In an open sort, the students must infer categories, sometimes creatively. This approach allows students to examine conceptual links among terms. It is most effective after the children have been exposed to the text and have become familiar with the meanings of the individual words.
Tier II Explicit Instruction		✓	This approach is useful with general vocabulary. Each word is written, pronounced, and defined in ordinary terms, including familiar synonyms. The teacher gives examples of correct usage in sentence contexts, one of which is a look-back to the text, and then asks students to contribute new sentence examples. The selected words are taught separately through this process because their meanings are unrelated. (For examples, note the author study unit on William Steig.)

FIGURE 6.6. Choosing an instructional method for vocabulary.

Comprehension Strategy	Procedural Knowledge	Sample Teacher Talk
Predicting	1. Look for clues in the words and pictures. 2. Think about what you already know about the topic. 3. On the basis of prior knowledge, predict what you think will happen.	Good readers predict before and during reading. Here I see a picture of a _____. I know that _____. Because of both what I see and what I know, I predict that this story will be about _____.
Monitoring, Questioning, and Re-Predicting	1. Keep the original prediction in mind. 2. Keep asking whether that prediction continues to make sense in light of new information from the text. 3. Use new information from the text and prior knowledge about that information to make new predictions.	I predicted that _____. So far, that might be right because the text says _____. I predicted that _____. That must not be true because the text says _____. My new prediction is _____.
Visualizing	1. Identify descriptive words the author is using. 2. Use prior knowledge about those words and about the world to create a visual image.	Good readers make pictures in their minds to help them to understand. I know that this story takes place _____. I know that setting would have _____. The author uses the words _____ and _____. In my mind I am visualizing _____.
Inferring	1. Note the clues embedded in the text. 2. Access your own experience regarding the clues. 3. Make inferences about the implied meaning based on experience and the clues the author provides.	The author tells us that this character is _____. Because of my own experience, I know that _____. Therefore, I think the character is _____.
Using Fix-Up Strategies	1. Stop when the text stops making sense. 2. Identify what is blocking meaning. 3. Think about what strategy you know that could be used to fix the problem. 4. Apply the strategy. 5. Test to see if the problem is fixed.	Wait. I thought that the text said _____. Here it says that _____. That doesn't make sense to me. I need to read ahead and see if the author tells me how both _____ and _____ could be true.

(continued)

FIGURE 6.7. Choosing an instructional method for comprehension.

Comprehension Strategy	Procedural Knowledge	Sample Teacher Talk
Discerning the Main Idea	1. Put yourself in the author's place. 2. Examine words and phrases for clues to what is important to the author. 3. Ask questions about what, in your experience, the clues combined seem to say about what the author values.	The author has given me a whole lot of facts about _____ and about _____. Some of them are the same and some are different. I think that the main idea here is that _____ are similar to _____ in some ways and different in other ways.
Retelling a Story	1. Know the parts of a story. 2. Review the book to identify the story information provided at the beginning, in the middle, and at the end.	I can use what I know about stories to retell this one very simply. I don't tell everything. I think about what the author usually does in the beginning, the middle, and the end. This story is set _____. The main characters are _____. The problem in the story is _____. The characters solve the problem by _____.
Synthesizing	1. Think about the content of each text. 2. Decide how they are alike and different. 3. Use experience about the common elements to create a synthesis.	When I want to think about two stories at once, I have to decide how they are alike and different. I first think about how they are alike. In our stories, they are alike because _____. Then I think about how they are different. Our stories are different because _____. Together, then, I can synthesize information from the stories to say that _____.

FIGURE 6.7. *(cont.)*

time comparing them. In this case, simple listing is combined with problem–solution and comparison–contrast.

An example of a popular trade book with multiple text structures that work well in combination is *Recycle!*, by Gail Gibbons (1992). She begins by describing the problem posed by ever-increasing amounts of trash. She does this by tracking the movement of trash from the curbside to the landfill, employing a sequential pattern to present the problem. She then turns to recycling as a major solution to this problem. However, the solution is broken down into the types of materials to be recycled. She uses simple listing to present them: paper, glass, cans, plastic, and polystyrene. A four-page section is devoted to each type. For this book, the overall text structure is problem–solution, but the problem component relies on a sequential structure and the solution component relies on simple listing. Although text structures can be complex, as the example of *Recycle!*

Basic Text Structure	Characteristics	Examples
Sequential	Events are described in the order they occur. In the case of fiction, these events usually follow a standard story format that centers on a problem that confronts the main character.	• A novel or story. • Historical events. • A process that may be repeated, such as the water cycle.
Topic–Subtopic	A major topic is addressed as a series of subtopics. The subtopics are often in no particular order.	• A book about France might include a section on its people, their language, their art, their industries, and so on.
Simple Listing	A major topic is addressed by considering its components. The components may be further subdivided. The components are not presented in a particular order—they are "simply listed."	• A book on rocks might be organized in three sections, one for each of the major types of rocks. Each type might include subsections on major examples. (The section on sedimentary rocks might include subsections on limestone and sandstone.)
Comparison–Contrast	Two or more concepts are presented by indicating how they are alike and different.	• A book on reptiles and amphibians would need to address how these groups are similar and how they differ.
Problem–Solution	The book centers around a major social or scientific problem and presents possible solutions.	• A book about air pollution might begin by defining the problem and then outline alternative approaches to contend with it.

FIGURE 6.8. Basic text structures used by trade book authors.

illustrates, pointing them out to students need not be. Doing so is an important part of introducing any book, especially nonfiction. There are two reasons for helping students recognize common text structures. The first is that building an awareness of them enhances comprehension. Familiar patterns enable students to make judgments about the content, predict what will come next, and arrive at inferences about the author's purpose. The second reason is that knowing about basic text structures helps students organize their writing. Accomplished writers never begin without some notion of how the finished product will be structured, and it is never too early to begin calling students' attention to these structures, even when the main target of small-group instruction is reading rather than writing.

STRATEGIES FOR EVERY PUPIL RESPONSE

As with our previous groups, it is vital that teachers monitor understanding and ensure high levels of engagement. An effective means of doing both is through every pupil

Technique	Description	Sample Teacher Talk
Signaled Hand Responses	Ask the children to use a hand gesture to indicate their response, making sure they cannot see one another's responses.	"Make a fist and put it on your chest. Show me one finger if you think … "
Written Responses	Ask the children to write down an answer. It could be only a word but could be more.	"On your paper, write the word *yes* if you think … or *no* if you think …"
Location in Book	Ask the children to locate a portion of the text that supports an answer. (Not useful for all grades.)	"Who can find a sentence that tells what the girl was thinking?"
Word Cards or List	Each student is given a list of words or a set of word cards. These are held up or pointed to by the students in response to questions.	"Point to the word that means …"
Share with Partner	Students turn to one another in pairs and share their responses.	"Tell your partner what you think …"

FIGURE 6.9. Every pupil response techniques for vocabulary and comprehension.

response techniques. Unlike the decoding-focused groups, however, we cannot depend heavily on manipulatives to accomplish this goal. Figure 6.9 presents some approaches that will work well for vocabulary and comprehension.

How Can We Design a Lesson?

We have explored the components of a vocabulary and comprehension small-group lesson, including the choice of books and methods. Next we consider how to organize these components into a complete lesson. We recommend a before–during–after approach, with the selected text serving as the centerpiece of each lesson. In the "before" phase, children are introduced to the text. The teacher describes the book and builds necessary background knowledge. The structure of the text is described, and in the case of nonfiction new terms are introduced. It is a good idea to suggest a focus for reading or listening. For example, the teacher might say, "Let's see if we can find out how dolphins breathe." In the "during" phase, the children encounter the text. For kindergarten and first grade, the teacher reads the selection aloud; for grades 2 and 3, the children read from their own copies. In the "after" phase, the teacher leads a discussion, grounded in questions that prompt the children to think actively about the text. For nonfiction texts, the discussion includes reviewing the technical vocabulary that the teacher introduced prior to reading. For fiction, the teacher now introduces several Tier 2 words. The discussion also includes a review of the comprehension strategy, prompted by appropriate questions. Figure 6.10 reflects this lesson format.

For short books, the before, during, and after phases might be completed during a single lesson. For longer books, the text will need to be broken up into segments. Each segment will need to be taught using the before–during–after approach, although what

Before	During	After
• Introduce the book. • For nonfiction, introduce key technical vocabulary. • Describe the text structure. • Provide a focus for reading (or listening) (e.g., "Let's see if we can find out … ").	• Read the selection aloud to K–1 children. • In K–1, the teacher pauses occasionally to make the read-aloud interactive. • Children in grades 2–3 read the selection in their own copies of the book.	• Review the comprehension strategy. • For nonfiction, review the technical vocabulary. • For fiction, introduce Tier 2 words. • Review the text structure. • Ask questions that prompt children to think actively about the text.

FIGURE 6.10. A before–during–after lesson format for vocabulary and comprehension.

happens during each phase will vary. For example, the before phase for the initial text segment will include introducing the book, but for the second segment this introduction could be replaced with a brief recap of the previous segment ("Let's see if we can remember what's happened so far."). For longer books, it will not suffice to plan a before, during, and after phase for the book as a whole. Each day's segment will need to be approached through a separate lesson plan.

TAKING STOCK

At the end of a 3-week cycle, the chief questions you need to answer are these.

1. Should any of these children be moved to a lower group? For children in grades 2 and 3, the issue is whether their fluency has remained at benchmark. For children in kindergarten and grade 1, the issue is whether their decoding development has continued to progress without the need for extra work in small groups.

2. Have the children responded to the books during this cycle by demonstrating adequate comprehension and by learning the meanings of the words introduced? This is actually a check on your book selection. If children have experienced difficulties with the books but have remained at acceptable levels in fluency or decoding, it may be necessary to reexamine your choice of books for the next 3-week cycle.

Various sources of evidence will help you reach these judgments. Remember that the chief issue is whether to alter your group memberships. Moving children from one group to another flexibly, in ways determined by the data you collect, is a hallmark of differentiation.

Step 1	Use student performance data to formulate (or reformulate) all groups.
Step 2	Choose a general focus for the 3-week cycle (e.g., dolphins).
Step 3	Select books for the entire cycle based on comparable difficulty but varied type.
Step 4	Choose one book from the set you have selected for a 3-week cycle.
Step 5	Analyze the book for vocabulary and text structure.
Step 6	Select a small number of key words and comprehension strategies.
Step 7	Consider whether graphic organizers will be useful for teaching vocabulary and/or text structure.
Step 8	Decide on instructional approaches that are suited to your goals.
Step 9	Build in opportunities for every pupil responses to monitor and engage.

FIGURE 6.11. Overall steps in planning a vocabulary and comprehension lesson.

SUMMARY

Planning small-group instruction for vocabulary and comprehension leads to a sequence of lessons, each centered around a trade book. Begin by forming a group on the basis of student performance. A set of books for the entire cycle, varying in type but similar in difficulty, is then selected, followed by lesson planning for each book. The steps in this process are outlined in Figure 6.11. Steps 4–9 are repeated for each book in the set.

LESSON PLANS

In the following pages, we present two sets of lesson plans based on readily available trade books. We designed each of the two sets around a 3-week cycle. One cycle is intended for K–1 read-alouds. It constitutes a thematic unit on sea mammals. The other cycle is intended to be read by second and third graders. It includes books by William Steig, winner of a Caldecott Medal and creator of *Shrek*. As in Chapters 3–5, we again stress that these lessons are not a complete curriculum. They are, however, ready to implement. You will see that our models include scripts for teacher talk. Our hope is that they adequately illustrate the ideas we have expressed in this chapter, such as the importance of balancing fiction and nonfiction, of introducing the books appropriately, and of employing effective techniques for building vocabulary knowledge and comprehension proficiency. In all of these ways, we intend them as models for the creation of similar 3-week units. As you plan those units, you will simply need to select the appropriate vocabulary and comprehension approaches; the need for scripts will fade.

K–1 Read-Aloud Cycle
Thematic Unit on Sea Mammals

Lesson 1
Dolphins, by Sylvia M. James (2002), Sections 1 and 2

	Before Reading
Introduce book or summarize to this point	In the next few days we are going to read some books about dolphins. Here is the first book. It was written by Sylvia James. On the cover you can see a picture of a dolphin. You may already know that a dolphin is an animal that lives in the ocean and looks like a big fish. But we will learn that a dolphin is not a fish.
Introduce key vocabulary	It will help us understand if we know the word *mammal*. Let me show you what a mammal is. [This is a concept-of-definition lesson. As you speak, create the diagram on a dry-erase board or chart paper.] A mammal is one kind of animal. It is an animal that has hair, breathes air, is warm-blooded, doesn't lay eggs, and whose babies drink milk. A dog is a mammal. A mouse is a mammal. A dolphin is a mammal. All of these animals have hair, breathe air, are warm-blooded, don't lay eggs, and have babies who drink milk. A lizard is not a mammal. It doesn't have hair. A fish is not a mammal. Baby fish don't drink milk. A bird is not a mammal. Birds lay eggs. The interesting thing about dolphins is that they are mammals that live in the ocean. Now that you know what a mammal is, you're ready to learn more about dolphins.
Describe text structure	When we are trying to use a book to learn about something new, we have to pay attention to the way the author is working with information. Sometimes authors have one main topic and several different subtopics. If we know that before we start reading, we can use it to help us remember the most important information. Here's how that looks. [Create this diagram as the children watch.]

(continued)

	(diagram)
Suggest a focus for reading	As I read the book to you, try to find out as much as you can about dolphins. You will learn about the sounds dolphins make and what their bodies are like. You will also learn about their babies.
During Reading	
Interactive approaches	[Pause after each two-page spread, ask children a question and have them share the answer with a partner.]
After Reading	
Review comprehension strategy	[Return to the diagram.] Remember that this author is writing about one main topic, dolphins. So far we have read about two subtopics. [Write them on the diagram and say them.) Tomorrow we will read about two more—four in all.

Lesson 2
Dolphins, by Sylvia M. James (2002), Sections 3 and 4

Before Reading	
Summarize the book to this point	Today we will finish our book about dolphins by Sylvia James. Yesterday we learned that a dolphin is not a fish but a mammal.
Review key vocabulary	Let's look again at our diagram that shows us what a mammal is. [Review the diagram.]
Describe text structure	You will also remember that Sylvia James has written about four subtopics in this book. So far we have read about two. [Review the diagram.]
Suggest a focus for reading	As I read the rest of the book to you, try to find out as much as you can about the sounds dolphins make and about baby dolphins. These are the last two subtopics.
During Reading	
Interactive approaches	[Pause after the third and fourth sections and ask each child to give a fact about that section.]
After Reading	
Review comprehension strategy	[Return to the text structure diagram.] Remember that this author is writing about one main topic, dolphins. We have now read about all four subtopics. Let's write them on our diagram together. [Write them on the diagram and say them.) Ask additional questions about dolphins.

(continued)

Lesson 3
Whales: Killer Whales, Blue Whales and More, by Deborah Hodge (1999), pp. 4–9

Before Reading	
Introduce book	Today we are going to start a book about whales. Here is the book. It was written by Deborah Hodge and illustrated by Pat Stephens. On the cover you can see a picture of one kind of whale. After reading our last book, you know that a dolphin is an animal that lives in the ocean and looks like a big fish. The same is true for a whale. Whales are not fish either. They are mammals.
Introduce key vocabulary	Let's review what we know about the word *mammal*. We made this chart to help us. [Show the diagram from Lessons 1 and 2.] Now we can add *whale* to our diagram. I could do it this way. [Add *whale* as a new link to the right of *dolphin*.] But wait. Dogs and mice live on land, right? And dolphins and whales live in the sea, right? So I could make a new diagram that looks like this. [Create the following.] Mammals → Land Mammals (Dog, Mouse), Sea Mammals (Dolphin, Whale) Today we will learn that there are two kinds of whales. Some have teeth and others don't. Whales that do not have teeth are called baleen whales. We can add these two kinds of whales to our diagram. [Add two branches under *whale*.] Whale → Toothed, Baleen
Describe text structure	Remember that when we are trying to use a book to learn about something new, we have to pay attention to the way the author is working with information. The author of our book about dolphins wrote about several subtopics. This book is organized the same way. If we know that before we start reading, we can use it to help us remember the most important information. You can see all the subtopics in the table of contents. [Display the table of contents and point to the subtopics.] Today we will read about toothed whales and baleen whales. Tomorrow, we'll move on to the next subtopic.
Suggest a focus for reading	As I read the book to you, try to find out as much as you can about these two kinds of whales. How are they the same? How are they different?

(continued)

During Reading	
Interactive approaches	[Pause after each section and ask children to signal their response to a question. For example, show one finger if they agree, two if they disagree.]

After Reading	
Review comprehension strategy and discuss new content	What is the biggest kind of whale? How big is a baby blue whale? The two kinds of whales catch their food in different ways. Who can tell me how? [Return to the table of contents.] Remember that this author is writing about one main topic, whales. So far we have read about two subtopics. [Refer the children back to the diagram.] Tomorrow we will read about three more. [Hold up the table of contents.] We'll learn where whales live, why they migrate (that is, why they move from place to place), and we'll learn about their bodies.

Lesson 4

Whales: Killer Whales, Blue Whales and More, by Deborah Hodge (1999), pp. 10–15

Before Reading	
Summarize book to this point	Today we are going to read some more of the book about whales. Last time we learned that there are two kinds of whales. Who remembers them? [Review tree diagram.]
Introduce key vocabulary	Today we will learn the parts of a whale's body. As I read, I will describe this picture. [Show pages 14 and 15.] We will learn where to find the whale's flukes, its tail, where its blowhole is, and where its fins are. You'll remember that dolphins have blowholes too. Where would you find a dolphin's blowhole?
Describe text structure	Remember that the author of our book about whales wrote about several subtopics. You can see all the subtopics in the table of contents. [Display the table of contents and point to the subtopics.] Today we will read about where whales live, why they migrate, and what their bodies are like.
Suggest a focus for reading	As I read the book to you, try to find out as much as you can about whales. See how much you can add to what you already know.

During Reading	
Interactive approaches	[Pause after each two-page spread, ask children a question, and have them share the answer with a partner.]

After Reading	
Review comprehension strategy and discuss new content	Why don't whales just stay in the warm waters all year? [Return to the table of contents.] Remember that this author is writing about one main topic, whales. Today we have read about these new subtopics. [Refer the children back to the table of contents.] Tomorrow we will read about more. We'll learn how whales move, what sounds they make, and what they eat.

(continued)

Lesson 5
Whales: Killer Whales, Blue Whales and More, by Deborah Hodge (1999), pp. 16–21

Before Reading	
Summarize book to this point	Today we are going to read some more of our book about whales. Last time we learned where whales live, why they migrate, and what their bodies are like.
Introduce key vocabulary	Today we will learn three ways that whales move. They have funny names, like spyhopping and flipper slapping. We will also learn about the food whales eat. It comes in different sizes, from giant squids to tiny krill.
Describe text structure	Remember that the author of our book about whales wrote about several subtopics. You can see all the subtopics in the table of contents. [Display the table of contents and point to the subtopics.] Today we will read about how whales move, what sounds they make, and what they eat.
Suggest a focus for reading	As I read the book to you, try to find out as much as you can about whales. See how much you can add to what you already know.
During Reading	
Interactive approaches	[Pause after each section and ask children to signal their response to a question. For example, show one finger if they agree, two if they disagree.]
After Reading	
Review comprehension strategy and discuss new content	The author says scientists don't know why whales breach. Why do you think? Why do baleen whales eat such tiny things? [Return to the table of contents.] Remember that this author is writing about one main topic, whales. Today we have read about these new subtopics. [Refer the children back to the table of contents.] Tomorrow we will read about more. We'll learn how whales are born, how they grow, and how they learn.

Lesson 6
Whales: Killer Whales, Blue Whales and More, by Deborah Hodge (1999), pp. 22–25

Before Reading	
Summarize book to this point	Today we are going to read some more of our book about whales. Last time we learned how whales move, what sounds they make, and what they eat.
Describe text structure	Remember that the author of our book about whales wrote about several subtopics. You can see all the subtopics in the table of contents. [Display the table of contents and point to the subtopics.] Today we will read about how whales are born, how they grow, and how they learn.
Suggest a focus for reading	As I read the book to you, try to find out as much as you can about whales. See how much you can add to what you already know. See if you can find out what a baby whale is called, where they rest when they're tired, and whether they like to play.
During Reading	
Interactive approaches	[Pause after each two-page spread, ask children a question, and have them share the answer with a partner.]

(continued)

After Reading	
Review comprehension strategy and discuss new content	The author says gray whale babies get tired easily. Do you think other kinds of whale babies do too? [Return to the table of contents.] Remember that this author is writing about one main topic, whales. Today we have read about these new subtopics. [Refer the children back to the table of contents.] Tomorrow we will read about two more subtopics. We'll learn how whales protect themselves and about whales and people.

Lesson 7
Whales: Killer Whales, Blue Whales and More, by Deborah Hodge (1999), pp. 26–29

Before Reading	
Summarize book to this point	Today we are going to read some more of our book about whales. Last time we learned how whales are born, how they grow, and how they learn.
Introduce key vocabulary	Today we will learn about a forest where whales sometimes hide. That's right—a forest! But this forest is underwater. It is made of tall seaweed called kelp.
Describe text structure	Remember that the author of our book about whales wrote about several subtopics. You can see all the subtopics in the table of contents. [Display the table of contents and point to the subtopics.] Today we will read about two more subtopics. Always remember that the table of contents can give you a quick idea of what you will find in an information book and how the author has organized the ideas.
Suggest a focus for reading	As I read some more of this book to you, try to find out even more about whales. See how much you can add to what you already know. See if you can find out how whales protect themselves. Also, see what you learn about how whales get along with humans.

During Reading	
Interactive approaches	[Pause after each section and ask children to signal their response to a question. For example, show one finger if they agree, two if they disagree.]

After Reading	
Review comprehension strategy and discuss new content	Do you think a killer whale might attack a blue whale? Is a dolphin a whale? [Return to the table of contents.] Remember that this author is writing about one main topic, whales. Today we have read about two more subtopics. [Refer the children back to the table of contents.] Let's count. There have been 13 subtopics in all. That's a lot of information, but the table of contents helps us remember how it is organized.

Lesson 8
Whales: Killer Whales, Blue Whales and More, by Deborah Hodge (1999), pages 30 and 31

Before Reading	
Summarize book to this point	Today we are going to read the rest of our book about whales. Last time we learned how whales protect themselves and how whales get along with humans.

(continued)

Introduce key vocabulary	Today we will review some of the important words we have learned about whales. We have already read these words. We will just go back and make sure we remember what they mean.
Describe text structure	Remember that the author of our book about whales wrote about several subtopics. You can see all the subtopics in the table of contents. [Display the table of contents and point to the subtopics.] Today we will read about the very last subtopic. Always remember that the table of contents can give you a quick idea of what you will find in an information book and how the author has organized the ideas.
Suggest a focus for reading	As I read the rest of this book to you, try to find out even more about whales. See how some people can tell which kind of whale they see just by looking at the tail.

During Reading	
Interactive approaches	[After reading page 30, call the children's attention to the question at the bottom of the page. The answer is upside-down. Ask children to signal their answers by a show of fingers.]

After Reading	
Review comprehension strategy and discuss new content	If you look just at the tails, which of these whales do you think has the smallest body? [Return to the table of contents.] Remember that this author is writing about one main topic, whales. Today we have read about the last subtopic—whale watching. [Refer the children back to the table of contents.]
Vocabulary review	Now we are going to review some of the words we have learned in this book. [This will be a concept sort.] The author has written them for us on the last page. [Display page 31.] I will say the word and what it means. [Quickly read the words and definitions, pointing them out as you go.] Now I will write some of these new words on the board. [Or chart paper.] I will also add a few of the other words from the book. [Write a column on the left side, as in the chart below. Pronounce each word as you write it.] Now, I think that some of these words go together. They have meanings that are related. Help me rewrite the words over here in groups that go together. [Prompt the students to group the words until they are arranged as you see them in the right-hand column of the figure.] Let's see if we can think of a name for each of these little groups of words. [The category names should be something like "types" and "parts."]

blubber baleen whale fluke toothed whale blowhole fin	blubber fluke blowhole fin baleen whale toothed whale

(continued)

Now let's go back to our diagram about whales and mammals. [Build the diagram below as you talk the children through it. Start at the top. Prompt participation as you do so.] You'll remember that we have been reading about mammals. Some live on land and others live in the sea. So far, we have read about two types of sea mammals—dolphins and whales. We also learned that there are two kinds of whales. Toothed whales use their teeth to catch prey. Baleen whales sift through the water for tiny plants and animals. One type of toothed whale is a killer whale. One type of baleen whale is a blue whale. We read about other types of whales, but I am not going to put them in my diagram because I don't have room.

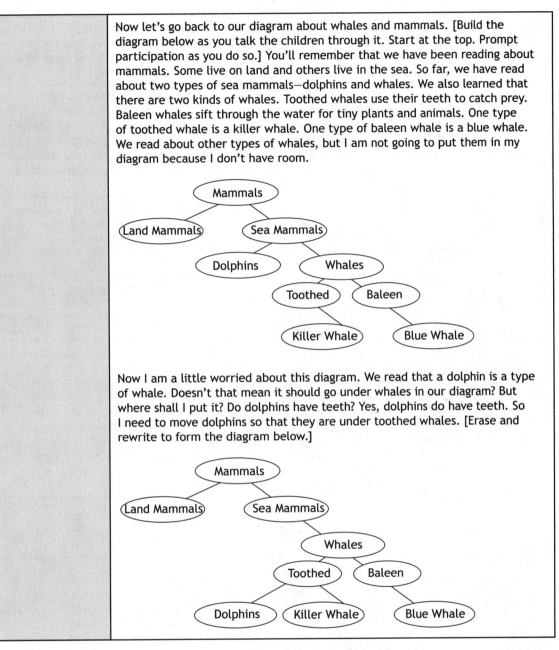

Now I am a little worried about this diagram. We read that a dolphin is a type of whale. Doesn't that mean it should go under whales in our diagram? But where shall I put it? Do dolphins have teeth? Yes, dolphins do have teeth. So I need to move dolphins so that they are under toothed whales. [Erase and rewrite to form the diagram below.]

Lesson 9
Killer Whales, by Seymour Simon (2002), through page beginning, "The male orca . . ."

Before Reading	
Introduce book	Today we are going to start a new book about just one kind of whale—the killer whale. Here is the book. It was written by Seymour Simon. On the cover you can see a picture of a killer whale. You will discover many interesting facts about them in this book.

(continued)

Introduce key vocabulary	Let's review our diagram about mammals. [Show the last diagram from Lesson 8.] Remember that killer whales are one type of toothed whale. You can see their teeth in the picture on the cover. In this book, you will meet some of the words you learned in the last book, like *fluke, fin,* and *flipper.*
Describe text structure	Remember that when we are trying to use a book to learn about something new, we have to pay attention to the way the author is working with information. The authors of the other two books wrote about several subtopics. This book is organized the same way. If we know that before we start reading, we can use it to help us remember the most important information. This book is very short, though, and there is no table of contents. Later, we'll see if we can decide what the subtopics are.
Suggest a focus for reading	As I read the first half of the book to you, try to find out as much as you can about killer whales. How big are they and what do they eat? How are they different from other whales? What is another name for them?
During Reading	
Interactive approaches	[Pause after each two-page spread, ask children a question, and have them share the answer with a partner.]
After Reading	
Review comprehension strategy and discuss new content	How do you think killer whales got their terrible name? What do scientists call them? Remember that Seymour Simon is writing about one main topic, killer whales. So far we have read about several subtopics. Let's see if we can figure out what they are. [Turn the pages as you go.] The book starts by giving us a few facts about killer whales. They are fast and can jump out of the water. Then we learn what they eat. (Not people, thank goodness!) Next we learn where they live. Then we read about what they look like, how big they are, and how they swim. Do you think that Seymour Simon could have made a table of contents? His subtopics are right there, aren't they? Now we know the secret of how he organized his ideas!

Lesson 10
Killer Whales, by Seymour Simon (2002), through end of book

Before Reading	
Summarize book	Today we are going to read the rest of our book about killer whales, or orcas. It was written by Seymour Simon. We have already discovered many interesting facts about them in this book. Who can tell me some of these facts?
Introduce key vocabulary	You already know that a baby whale is called a calf. Today we will read that a female is called a cow and a male is called a bull. Just like cattle!
Describe text structure	Remember that when we are trying to use a book to learn about something new, we have to pay attention to the way the author is working with information. Seymour Simon has written about several subtopics, but because this book is short, there is no table of contents. Yesterday we figured out the subtopics in the first half of the book. Today, we'll see if we can decide what the rest of the subtopics are.

(continued)

Suggest a focus for reading	As I read the second half of the book to you, see what else you can find out about killer whales. How do they find their way through dark water? How do they hunt? How many orcas are in a pod?
During Reading	
Interactive approaches	[Pause after each two-page spread and ask children to signal their response to a question. For example, show one finger if they agree, two if they disagree.]
After Reading	
Review comprehension strategy and discuss new content	How do orcas find their way through dark water? How do they hunt? How many orcas are in a pod? Remember that Seymour Simon is writing about one main topic, killer whales. Today we have read about more subtopics. Let's see if we can figure out what they are. [Turn the pages as you go.] First we read about how they find their way in cloudy water. Then we found out how they hunt. Then we learned how big their pods are. Next we learned about baby orcas. Then we read about how high they can breach and how some of them live in marine life parks. Do you still think that Seymour Simon could have made a table of contents? Yes, his subtopics are still right there, aren't they? He writes about one subtopic after another.

Lesson 11
Baby Whales Drink Milk, by Barbara Juster Esbensen (1994), through page 11

Before Reading	
Introduce book	Today we are going to read a new book about sea mammals. It is called *Baby Whales Drink Milk,* by Barbara Juster Esbensen. Look at the picture on the cover. The baby whale is swimming very close to its mother.
Introduce key vocabulary	This book tells about baby humpback whales. Let's look at our diagram of mammals to see where humpbacks belong. [Reconstruct the diagram from Lesson 8, talking the children through it as a review.] Now, if a humpback is a whale, it must go under whales. That means it must go . . . where? But should I put it with the toothed whales, like dolphins and killer whales, down here, or should I put humpbacks with the baleen whales, like blue whales, over here? We don't know yet, do we?

(continued)

Describe text structure	Remember that when we are trying to use a book to learn about something new, we have to pay attention to the way the author is working with information. Barbara Esbensen has an interesting way of telling us about baby humpback whales. There is no table of contents. [Demonstrate.] There is no topic or subtopics. Instead, she tells how whale babies are like other baby mammals. That means that they drink milk, and this book is about how they do it. But Barbara Esbensen also gives us many facts about whales as we read. Some of the facts you know. Others will be new.
Suggest a focus for reading	As I read the first part of the book to you, see what you can learn about humpbacks. How long does a baby humpback live inside its mother? Does its mother like warm or cold water when her baby is born?
During Reading	
Interactive approaches	[Pause after each two-page spread, ask children a question, and have them share the answer with a partner. Look for chances to refer to the previous three books in this cycle.]
After Reading	
Review comprehension strategy and discuss new content	Let's see if we can answer some questions about humpback babies. Put your hand on your chest. Wait until I say "go." If you think a humpback baby grows inside its mother for over a year before it is born, show me one finger. If you think a humpback baby grows inside its mother for almost a year before it is born, show me two fingers. Ready? Go. [Confirm by rereading the first sentence on page 10.] Now, hand on chest again. Wait until I say "go." If you think a humpback mother likes warm water to have her baby, show me one finger. If you think a humpback mother likes cold water to have her baby, show me two fingers. Ready? Go. [Confirm by rereading the last sentence on page 11.] Have we found out yet whether humpbacks have teeth? [No.] Maybe we'll find out tomorrow! Until we know, we can't finish our diagram.

Lesson 12
Baby Whales Drink Milk, by Barbara Juster Esbensen (1994), pp. 12–18

Before Reading	
Summarize book to this point	Today we are going to read the second part of our book, called *Baby Whales Drink Milk*, by Barbara Juster Esbensen. So far we have been learning about humpbacks and their babies. Who can remember what we learned?
Introduce key vocabulary	Like other whales, humpbacks have blowholes, but you might be surprised at how many they have. When they breathe out, air and water shoot up high into the air. This is called spouting. Today we will also learn that whales, like all mammals, are warm-blooded. You will find out what that means. It is just one of the ways that you are like a whale.
Describe text structure	Remember that Barbara Esbensen has an interesting way of telling us about humpbacks. She shows us pictures about one humpback mother and her baby, but along the way she gives us many facts that are true for all whales.
Suggest a focus for reading	Today we will learn many new facts about humpbacks. For example, see if you can find out how many blowholes a humpback has. You should also be able to tell me what it means to be warm-blooded. Most important, you will find out how a baby humpback gets milk from its mother.

(continued)

During Reading	
Interactive approaches	[Pause after each two-page spread and ask children to signal their response to a question. For example, show one finger if they agree, two if they disagree.]

After Reading	
Review comprehension strategy and discuss new content	Remember that this book gives us many facts. Let's see if we can remember them. Put your hand on your chest. Wait until I say "go." Show me the number of fingers that is the same as the number of blowholes a humpback has. Ready? Go. [Confirm by rereading the last paragraph on page 12.] Now, hand on chest again. Wait until I say "go." If you think a humpback is cold-blooded like a fish, show me one finger. If you think a humpback is warm-blooded like a human, show me two fingers. Ready? Go. [Confirm by rereading the first paragraph on page 18.] What else did we learn about humpbacks today? [Prompt recall and distribute opportunities.] Have we found out yet whether humpbacks have teeth? [No.] Maybe we'll find out tomorrow! Until we know, we can't finish our diagram.

Lesson 13

Baby Whales Drink Milk, by Barbara Juster Esbensen (1994), pp. 21–28 (skip facts on pages 30 and 31)

Before Reading	
Summarize book to this point	Today we are going to read the last part of our book, called *Baby Whales Drink Milk*, by Barbara Juster Esbensen. We have been following the mother and her baby. Who can remember some of the things we've learned so far? [Lead a brief review.]
Introduce key vocabulary	Today, we will learn that humpbacks eat small animals called krill. [Write this word on chart paper or a white board.] You saw this word in one of our other books. You will finally learn whether humpbacks are baleen or toothed whales. [Write these two words.]
Describe text structure	Remember that Barbara Esbensen has an interesting way of telling us about humpbacks. She shows us pictures about one humpback mother and her baby, but along the way she gives us many facts that are true for all whales.
Suggest a focus for reading	As I read, pay attention to whether humpbacks are toothed or baleen whales. You will also find out if they can make sounds and where they spend the summer. You will even find out if they have hair. Let's make some predictions. Put your hand on your chest. When I say "go," show me one finger if you think humpback whales have hair and two fingers if you think they do not have hair. Ready? Go. Let's try another one. Put your hand on your chest. When I say "go," show me one finger if you think humpback whales can make sounds and two fingers if you think they cannot make sounds. Ready? Go. OK, one more time. Put your hand on your chest. When I say "go," show me one finger if you think humpbacks are baleen whales and two fingers if you think they are toothed whales. Ready? Go. Now we will find out if your predictions are right.

During Reading	
Interactive approaches	[Pause after each two-page spread and ask children to signal their response to a question. For example, show one finger if they agree, two if they disagree.]

(continued)

	After Reading
Review comprehension strategy and discuss new content	Remember that this is a book that has many facts. We tried to predict some of them today. Let's see if you were right or wrong. Who predicted that humpbacks have hair? [Confirm by rereading page 21.] Who predicted that humpbacks can make sounds? [Confirm by rereading page 23.] Who predicted that humpbacks are baleen whales? [Confirm by rereading page 26.] Sometimes our predictions are wrong, but that's OK. They give us a reason to read carefully. Now that we know that humpbacks are baleen whales, we can put them in our diagram. [Display the diagram.] Help me decide where to write the word *humpback*. 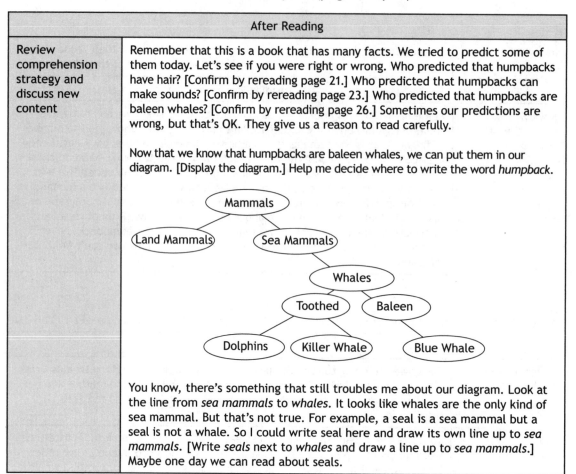 You know, there's something that still troubles me about our diagram. Look at the line from *sea mammals* to *whales*. It looks like whales are the only kind of sea mammal. But that's not true. For example, a seal is a sea mammal but a seal is not a whale. So I could write seal here and draw its own line up to *sea mammals*. [Write *seals* next to *whales* and draw a line up to *sea mammals*.] Maybe one day we can read about seals.

Lesson 14
Review and Synthesis

Today we are going to review what we have learned about sea mammals. Together we have read these four books. [Display and say titles and authors.] Let's make a chart that tells some of the information we know about them. I have already listed some of the mammals here on the left. Across the top I have written some words that may or may not be true for each one. You can help me decide. I will put a plus sign if the word is true and a minus sign if it is not true. The first mammal is the blue whale. Because the blue whale is a type of whale I will put a plus sign here. Now, does the blue whale eat other whales? Show me one finger if you think so and two fingers if you don't think so. [Complete the feature analysis chart in this way.]

Mammal	Is a Whale	Babies Drink Milk	Eats Whales	Lives in Saltwater	Eats Plants
blue whale	+	+	–	+	+
humpback	+	+	–	+	–
killer whale	+	+	+	+	–
dolphin	+	+	–	+	–

[Encourage the children to look for patterns and make comparisons. For example, all four have babies that drink milk because all are mammals. Also, the whales all live in saltwater. Reconstruct the tree diagram. This time solicit help for where to put each new word. Include whale names not previously included.]

Author Study Cycle for Grades 2–3 (Fiction)
William Steig

Lesson 1
Shrek! (2001), Part 1 (through the page where Shrek heats his dinner)

	Before Reading
Introduce author and first book	Today we are going to begin reading some books by William Steig. William Steig was a famous artist, who wrote many books for children. He wrote the words *and* he also illustrated his books. Most of William Steig's books are fantasy. A fantasy is a piece of fiction that has at least one part that is impossible. It could involve magic or science that isn't possible. Other than that, fantasy has the characteristics that you know: a setting, characters, a problem, a series of events that stem from the problem, and a solution. Great fantasy also has a theme—a deep message or lesson that goes beyond the story.
	Our first book is *Shrek*. You may already know something about the kind monster named Shrek, but it will be interesting to read the original story.
Describe text structure	Here is a story map that you can use as you read *Shrek*. This book tells a story by describing one event after another, but William Steig begins by telling us about Shrek and his parents. A story map can help us understand how the story is written.
Suggest a focus for reading	As you read the first part of this book, use your story map to make sure that your understanding is on target. You can use the map to take notes. [Distribute a blank story map.] You'll need to save some room because we'll read some more of this book tomorrow. Today read through this page. [Have each child turn to the page showing Shrek heating his dinner.] Now begin reading. If you have trouble with a word, try to figure out what it means from the way it is used in the sentence.
	During Reading
	[Monitor as children read.]
	After Reading
Review comprehension strategy	[Return to the story map.] Let's look at our story maps. They can help us summarize what has happened so far. [Ask questions that take the children through the map.] Tomorrow we'll start at this point. Show me one finger if you think that Shrek will go back home and two fingers if you think he'll continue on his journey. Tomorrow we'll find out. [Collect the story maps.]
Teach Tier 2 Words	Now let's look at some new words. Turn to this page. [Indicate the first page.] Our first word is *instantly*. What word? *Instantly* means right away. "A snake dumb enough to bite him *instantly* got convulsions and died." What would I want you to do if I asked you to come here instantly? *Instantly* means right away. The second word is *specialized*. What word? *Specialize* means to learn just one thing until you are an expert. [Indicate the page with the witches.] "The witch *specialized* in horrors." A doctor might specialize in one part of the body, like the brain or the skin. *Specialize* means to learn just one thing until you are an expert.

(continued)

Lesson 2
Shrek!, Part 2 (through the page with the dragon)

Before Reading	
Review book to this point	Today we are going to read the next part of *Shrek*, by William Steig. Remember that this book is a fantasy. A fantasy is a piece of fiction that has at least one part that is impossible. Who can tell me some impossible things about *Shrek*?
Suggest a focus for reading	Here are your story maps. As you read some more, be sure to jot down the events of the story. Also, remember that yesterday we predicted whether Shrek would continue or turn back. Read to see if you were right. Today read through this page. [Have each child turn to the page showing the dragon.] Now begin reading. If you have trouble with a word, try to figure out what it means from the way it is used in the sentence.

During Reading	
	[Monitor as children read.]

After Reading	
Review comprehension strategy	[Return to the story map.] Let's look at our story maps. They can help us summarize what has happened so far. [Ask questions that take the children through the map.] Tomorrow we'll start at this point. [Collect the story maps.]
Teach Tier 2 Words	Now let's look at some new words. Turn to this page. [Indicate the page where Shrek eats lightning.] Our first word is *disgusting*. What word? *Disgusting* means bad mannered or gross. "Did you ever see somebody so *disgusting*?" Can you think of something disgusting? I think picking your nose is disgusting. *Disgusting* means bad mannered or gross. The second word is *separate*. What word? *Separate* means to put things into different places. [Indicate the page with the dragon.] "The irascible dragon was preparing to *separate* Shrek from his noggin." I might separate the change in my purse into pennies, nickels, dimes, and quarters. *Separate* means to put things into different places.

Lesson 3
Shrek!, Part 3 (through the page showing the knight with his sword raised)

Before Reading	
Review book to this point	Today we are going to read the next part of *Shrek*, by William Steig. Remember that this book is a fantasy. A fantasy is a piece of fiction that has at least one part that is impossible. Who can tell me some more impossible things about *Shrek*?
Suggest a focus for reading	Here are your story maps. As you read some more, be sure to jot down the events of the story.

During Reading	
	[Monitor as children read.]

(continued)

148

After Reading	
Review comprehension strategy	[Return to the story map.] Let's look at our story maps. They can help us summarize what has happened so far. [Ask questions that take the children through the map.] Tomorrow we'll start at this point. [Collect the story maps.]
Teach Tier 2 Words	Now let's look at some new words. Turn to this page. [Indicate the first page with the donkey.] Our first word is *wandered*. What word? To *wander* means to travel without any place to go. "Shrek *wandered* on." Do you think it might be fun to just wander? To *wander* means to travel without any place to go. The second word is *shrieked*. What word? *Shriek* means to cry out loudly. [Indicate the second page with the donkey.] "Shrek *shrieked*." A person might shriek if he or she sees a mouse. *Shriek* means to cry out loudly.

Lesson 4
Shrek!, Part 4 (through the end of the book)

Before Reading	
Review book to this point	Today we are going to finish *Shrek*, by William Steig. First, let's review what's happened so far. We'll do this very quickly, just to sum up. I'll tell one event and you tell what happened next. First, Shrek's parents made him leave home. What happened next? [Continue in this way, allowing the children to look back through their copies.]
Suggest a focus for reading	Here are your story maps. As you read the rest of the book, be sure to jot down the events of the story. You will also find out how the story turns out. This story has a surprise ending, which means it's very hard to predict what happened. Would anyone like to guess?
During Reading	
	[Monitor as children read.]
After Reading	
Review comprehension strategy	[Return to the story map.] Let's look at our story maps. They can help us summarize what has happened in the last part of the story. [Ask questions that take the children through the map.] Now, what about the ending? Did you like it? Were you surprised? Would you have ended it differently?
Teach Tier 2 Words	Now let's look at some of the new words. Turn to this page. [Indicate the first page with mirrors.] Our first word is *hideous*. What word? *Hideous* means very ugly. "All around him were hundreds of *hideous* creatures." Can you think of an animal that looks hideous? *Hideous* means very ugly. The second word is *appalled*. What word? *Appalled* means shocked or surprised at something very bad. [Indicate the same page.] "He was so *appalled* he could barely manage to spit a bit of flame." You might be appalled if someone said something unkind. *Appalled* means shocked or surprised at something very bad.

(continued)

Lesson 5
Doctor De Soto (1992), Part 1 (through the page where Doctor De Soto washes his hands)

Before Reading	
Introduce second book	Today we are going to begin our second book by William Steig. It is called *Doctor De Soto*. Remember that William Steig wrote *and* illustrated his books. Like *Shrek!*, *Doctor De Soto* is a fantasy. A fantasy is a piece of fiction that has at least one part that is impossible. Doctor De Soto was a mouse who was a dentist. As you can see from his picture, he was very sure of himself. [Have children examine the cover.] I think you'll agree that it is impossible for a mouse to be a dentist, but we can have fun imagining that it's true.
Describe text structure	Here is a story map that you can use as you read *Doctor De Soto*. Just like *Shrek*, this book tells a story by describing one event after another, but first we learn how Doctor De Soto works as a dentist. Then we will find out about an important problem he has to solve. A story map can help us understand how the story is written.
Suggest a focus for reading	As you read the first part of this book, use your story map to make sure that your understanding is on target. You can use the map to take notes. [Distribute a blank story map.] You'll need to save some room because we'll read some more of this book tomorrow. Today read through this page. [Have each child turn to the page showing Doctor De Soto washing his hands.] Now begin reading. If you have trouble with a word, try to figure out what it means from the way it is used in the sentence.
During Reading	
	[Monitor as children read.]
After Reading	
Review comprehension strategy	[Return to the story map.] Let's look at our story maps. How did Doctor De Soto treat large animals? Which animals do the pictures show him treating? Why does Doctor De Soto tell the fox he can't treat him? Is a fox really dangerous? Why does Doctor De Soto decide to let the fox in? Tomorrow we'll start at this point. You can see the problem he faces. He wants to help the poor fox but he doesn't want to be eaten. It looks like he has decided to treat the fox, but he might change his mind. We can use what we already know to make a prediction as we read. We might be wrong, but we can try. Show me one finger if you think that Doctor De Soto will really go ahead and treat the fox, or show me two fingers if you think he'll change his mind. Tell me why you think so. [Discuss reasons.] Tomorrow we'll find out. [Collect the story maps.]
Teach Tier 2 Words	Now let's look at some new words. Turn to this page. [Indicate the first page.] Our first word is *regular*. What word? *Regular* means usual or what happens most of the time. "Those close to his own size—moles, chipmunks, et cetera—sat in the *regular* dentist's chair." Most people put regular gas in their cars. *Regular* means usual or what happens most of the time. The second word is *assistant*. What word? An *assistant* is a helper. [Indicate the second page.] "Doctor De Soto was hoisted up to the patient's mouth by his *assistant*." Sometimes I ask one of my students to be my assistant. An *assistant* is a helper.

(continued)

Lesson 6
Doctor De Soto, Part 2 (through the page where Doctor De Soto is lying in bed)

Before Reading	
Review book to this point	Today we are going to continue reading *Doctor De Soto*, by William Steig. First, let's review what's happened so far. We'll do this very quickly, just to sum up. I'll tell one event and you tell what happened next. First, a fox came with a toothache. What happened next? [Continue in this way, allowing the children to look back through their copies.]
Suggest a focus for reading	Here are your story maps. As you read the next part of the book, be sure to jot down the events of the story. Today you will find out whether Doctor De Soto decides to help the fox. It would be very dangerous for him to do that. Read to see if your prediction was right. You will also learn that Doctor De Soto has a new problem. Read to find out what it is.
During Reading	
	[Monitor as children read.]
After Reading	
Review comprehension strategy	[Return to the story map.] Let's look at our story maps. They can help us summarize what has happened so far. [Ask questions that take the children through the map.] Now, how many of you were surprised that Doctor De Soto decided to help the fox? What is the new problem he faces? What advice would you give him? Can you guess what his plan might be? Tomorrow we'll find out. [Collect the story maps.]
Teach Tier 2 Words	Now let's look at some new words. Turn to this page. [Indicate the page where Doctor De Soto steps into the fox's mouth.] Our first word is *announce*. What word? *Announce* means to tell people something important. " `This tooth will have to come out,' Doctor De Soto *announced*." Every day here in school someone announces something on the intercom. *Announce* means to tell people something important. The second word is *misery*. What word? *Misery* means feeling great pain. [Indicate the next page.] "Despite his *misery*, he realized he had a tasty little morsel in his mouth." If you hurt yourself badly you would be in misery for awhile. *Misery* means feeling great pain.

Lesson 7
Doctor De Soto, Part 3 (through the end of the book)

Before Reading	
Review book to this point	Today we are going to finish reading *Doctor De Soto*, by William Steig. First, let's review what happened last time. We'll do this very quickly, just to sum up. I'll tell one event and you tell what happened next. I remember that Doctor De Soto climbed up a ladder and looked in the fox's mouth. What happened next? [Continue in this way, allowing the children to look back through their copies.]
Suggest a focus for reading	Here are your story maps. As you read the last part of the book, be sure to jot down the rest of the events in the story. Today you will find out what Doctor De Soto's plan was and you will see if it works. Read to find out if the plan works.

(continued)

During Reading	
	[Monitor as children read.]

After Reading	
Review comprehension strategy	[Return to the story map.] Let's look at our story maps. They can help us summarize what has happened so far. [Ask questions that take the children through the map.] Now, who can tell me about Doctor De Soto's plan? Did you like the ending? Were you surprised? Would you have ended the book differently?
Teach Tier 2 Words	Now let's look at some new words. Turn to this page. [Indicate the page where the fox tips his cap.] Our first word is *promptly*. What word? *Promptly* means right on time. "The next morning, *promptly* at eleven, a very cheerful fox turned up." I love it when my students arrive promptly each morning. *Promptly* means right on time. The second word is *lug*. What word? *Lug* means to carry something heavy. [Indicate the next page.] "His wife was *lugging* the heavy tooth up the ladder." Sometimes I have to lug lots of things from my car. *Lug* means to carry something heavy.

Lesson 8
Amos and Boris (1977), Part 1 (through the page beginning, "And there he was.")

Before Reading	
Introduce third book	Today we are going to begin our third book by William Steig. It is called *Amos and Boris*. Remember that William Steig wrote the words *and* drew the pictures for his books. Like *Shrek!* and *Doctor De Soto*, *Amos and Boris* is a fantasy. A fantasy is a piece of fiction that has at least one part that is impossible. Like Doctor De Soto, Amos was a mouse, but he was not a dentist. As you can see from the picture on the cover, he sailed in a boat. [Have children examine the cover.] I think you'll agree that it is impossible for a mouse to be a sailor, and that is just one of the impossible things that make this story a fantasy. For example, we will learn that Amos not only sailed in a boat, but that he built the boat himself.
Describe text structure	Here is a story map that you can use as you read *Amos and Boris*. Just like *Shrek!* and *Doctor De Soto*, this book tells a story by describing one event after another, but first we find out why Amos wanted to sail away. Then we will find out how he built his boat. A story map can help us understand how the story is written.
Suggest a focus for reading	As you read the first part of this book, use your story map to make sure that you understand. Remember to use the map to take notes. [Distribute a blank story map.] You'll need to save some room because we'll read some more of this book tomorrow. Today read through this page. [Have each child turn to the page beginning, "And there he was."] Now begin reading. If you have trouble with a word, try to figure out what it means from the way it is used in the sentence.

During Reading	
	[Monitor as children read.]

(continued)

After Reading	
Review comprehension strategy	[Return to the story map.] Let's look at our story maps. Why did Amos want to sail away? What are some of the things he took with him on his boat? Would you have taken these same things? How did Amos leave his boat? Tomorrow we'll start at this point. You can see the problem he faces. He is swimming alone in the middle of the ocean. It looks like he may drown. We can use what we already know to make a prediction as we read. We might be wrong, but we can try. Put your fist on your chest. When I say "go," show me one finger if you think that Amos will drown. Show me two fingers if you think he will be rescued, or show me three fingers if you think he'll make it to shore by himself. Tell me why you think so. [Discuss reasons.] Tomorrow we'll find out. [Collect the story maps.]
Teach Tier 2 Words	Now let's look at some new words. Turn to this page. [Indicate the third page.] Our first word is *mend*. What word? *Mend* means to fix something by sewing it. "A needle and thread for the *mending* of torn sails." I mend my clothes when a button comes off. *Mend* means to fix something by sewing it. The second word is *immense*. What word? *Immense* means very big or very much. [Indicate the page where Amos is atop a wave.] "He was enjoying his trip *immensely*." That's really an immense wave too, isn't it? *Immense* means very big or very much.

Lesson 9
Amos and Boris, Part 2 (through the page beginning, "They became the closest possible friends.")

Before Reading	
Review book to this point	Today we are going to read the next part of *Amos and Boris*, by William Steig. Remember that this book is a fantasy. A fantasy is a piece of fiction that has at least one part that is impossible. Who can remind us of some of the impossible things about this book?
Suggest a focus for reading	Here are your story maps. As you read some more, be sure to jot down the events of the story. Remember your predictions from last time. Let's read to see who was right. Today read through this page. [Have each child turn to the page beginning, "They became the closest possible friends."] Now begin reading. If you have trouble with a word, try to figure out what it means from the way it is used in the sentence.

During Reading	
	[Monitor as children read.]

After Reading	
Review comprehension strategy	[Return to the story map.] Let's look at our story maps. They can help us summarize what has happened so far. [Ask questions that take the children through the map.] Tomorrow we'll start at this point. [Collect the story maps.]
Teach Tier 2 Words	Now let's look at some new words. Turn to this page. [Indicate the page where the whale first appears.] Our first word is *dreadful*. What word? *Dreadful* refers to something you do not like. "As he was asking himself these *dreadful* questions." I think that traffic can sometimes be dreadful. *Dreadful* refers to something you do not like. The second word is *attend*. What word? *Attend* means to come to a place where others are meeting. [Indicate the next page.] "To *attend* a meeting of whales from all the seven seas." I'm so happy that all of you decided to attend school today. *Attend* means to come to a place where others are meeting.

(continued)

Lesson 10
Amos and Boris, Part 3 (through the end of the book)

Before Reading	
Review book to this point	Today we are going to read the rest of *Amos and Boris*, by William Steig. Remember that this book is a fantasy. A fantasy is a piece of fiction that has at least one part that is impossible. A mouse and a whale cannot really talk, or build boats, or be friends. Those things are fun for us to think about, but they're also impossible.
Suggest a focus for reading	Here are your story maps. As you read to the end, be sure to jot down the final events of the story. Remember that Boris helped Amos when he was in trouble. Now it is Amos's turn to help Boris. Do you think a mouse can really help a whale? Maybe not in real life, but remember that this is a fantasy. Anything can happen. Now begin reading to find out how Amos saves Boris's life. If you have trouble with a word, try to figure out what it means from the way it is used in the sentence.
During Reading	
	[Monitor as children read.]
After Reading	
Review comprehension strategy	[Return to the story map.] Let's look at our story maps. They can help us summarize what has happened in the whole story. [Ask questions that take the children through the map.] How did Amos help Boris? Why was Amos sad?
Teach Tier 2 Words	Now let's look at some new words. Turn to this page. [Indicate the page where the whale is on the beach.] Our first word is *desperate*. What word? *Desperate* means needing help right away. "Boris was lying high and dry on the sand, losing his moisture in the hot sun and needing *desperately* to be put back in the water." A person who is in trouble might be desperate for help. *Desperate* means needing help right away. The second word is *pity*. What word? *Pity* means feeling sorry for someone. [Indicate the next page.] "Amos gazed at Boris in an agony of *pity*." I think we would pity someone if something bad happened to them. *Pity* means feeling sorry for someone.

Lesson 11
Brave Irene (1986), Part 1 (through the page beginning, "When she reached the Apple Road . . . ")

Before Reading	
Introduce fourth book	Today we are going to begin our fourth book by William Steig. It is called *Brave Irene*. Remember that William Steig wrote the words *and* drew the pictures for his books. But this book is not like *Shrek*, or *Doctor De Soto*, or *Amos and Boris*. *Brave Irene* isn't really a fantasy. A fantasy is a piece of fiction that has at least one part that is impossible. In *Brave Irene*, all of the events could happen. In this book, a dressmaker's daughter, named Irene, wants to take a new dress to a very rich woman. She is a duchess, which is almost like a queen. It will be a hard trip because it's snowing. Now that doesn't sound impossible, does it?
Describe text structure	Here is a story map that you can use as you read *Brave Irene*. Just like the other three books, this one tells a story by describing one event after another, but first we meet Irene and her mother. A story map can help us understand how the story is written.

(continued)

Suggest a focus for reading	As you read the first part of this book, use your story map to make sure that you understand. Remember to use the map to take notes. [Distribute a blank story map.] You'll need to save some room because we'll read some more of this book tomorrow. Today read through this page. [Have each child turn to the page beginning, "When she reached Apple Road . . ."] See if you can find out why Irene decides to go out alone in a snow storm. You will learn how hard it was to walk through that storm. Now begin reading. If you have trouble with a word, try to figure out what it means from the way it is used in the sentence.
	During Reading
	[Monitor as children read.]
	After Reading
Review comprehension strategy	[Return to the story map.] Let's look at our story maps. Why did Irene decide to go out in the storm? Why was it so hard to travel through the storm? Tomorrow we'll start at this point. You can see the problem Irene faces. It is dangerous to go on. What do you predict she will do? Will she turn back or keep going? Can you get a hint from the title of the book? Remember, we can use what we already know to make a prediction as we read. We might be wrong, but we can try. Put your fist on your chest. When I say "go," show me one finger if you think that Irene will turn back. Show me two fingers if you think she will keep going, or show me three fingers if you think something different will happen. Tell me why you think so. [Discuss reasons.] Tomorrow we'll find out. [Collect the story maps.]
Teach Tier 2 Words	Now let's look at some new words. Turn to this page. [Indicate the first page.] Our first word is *manage*. What word? *Manage* means to do something very hard. "Mrs. Bobbin, the dressmaker, was tired and had a bad headache, but she still *managed* to sew the last stitches in the gown she was making." I know that each of you can manage to learn something new even if you have to work hard. *Manage* means to do something very hard. The second word is *splendid*. What word? *Splendid* means wonderful. [Indicate the third page.] "With great care, Irene took the *splendid* gown down from the dummy and packed it in a big box." I think it would be splendid if we could read more books by William Steig. *Splendid* means wonderful.

Lesson 12
Brave Irene, Part 2 (through the page beginning, "Irene pushed forward . . .")

	Before Reading
Review book to this point	Today we are going to read the next part of *Brave Irene*, by William Steig. Remember that this book really isn't a fantasy. The events it tells might really have taken place. Who can remind us of what's happened so far?
Suggest a focus for reading	Here are your story maps. As you read some more, be sure to jot down the events of the story. Remember your predictions from last time. Let's read to see who was right. Will Irene turn back or keep going? Today read through this page. [Have each child turn to the page beginning, "Irene pushed forward . . ."] Now begin reading. If you have trouble with a word, try to figure out what it means from the way it is used in the sentence.
	During Reading
	[Monitor as children read.]

(continued)

After Reading	
Review comprehension strategy	[Return to the story map.] Let's look at our story maps. They can help us summarize what has happened so far. [Ask questions that take the children through the map.] Irene is in real trouble now. She's almost buried in the snow. Will she be all right? Tomorrow we'll start at this point and find out. [Collect the story maps.]
Teach Tier 2 Words	Now let's look at some new words. Turn to this page. [Indicate the page with the stump.] Our first word is *plod*. What word? *Plod* means to walk when you are very tired. "She went *plodding* on." If we walk two miles we might start out quickly but I think we'd be plodding by the end. *Plod* means to walk when you are very tired. The second word is *clutch*. What word? *Clutch* means to hold something tightly. [Indicate the next page.] "She shoved her way through it, *clutching* the empty box." When I'm in a crowd, I always make sure to clutch my purse. *Clutch* means to hold something tightly.

Lesson 13
Brave Irene, Part 3 (through the end of the book)

Before Reading	
Review book to this point	Today we are going to read the rest of *Brave Irene*, by William Steig. Remember that this book is not a fantasy. The events might really have happened. Who can tell me where we left off?
Suggest a focus for reading	Here are your story maps. As you read to the end, be sure to jot down the final events of the story. Remember that Irene was in big trouble. She was trying to reach the duchess but is nearly buried in snow. Now begin reading to find out how she escapes the snow and reaches the duchess. If you have trouble with a word, try to figure out what it means from the way it is used in the sentence.
During Reading	
	[Monitor as children read.]
After Reading	
Review comprehension strategy	[Return to the story map.] Let's look at our story maps. They can help us summarize what has happened in the whole story. [Ask questions that take the children through the map.] How did Irene reach the duchess? How did the people in the palace treat Irene? What gift did the duchess send to Irene's mother?
Teach Tier 2 Words	Now let's look at some new words. Turn to this page. [Indicate the page with the fireplace.] Our first word is *fret*. What word? *Fret* means to worry. " `Don't *fret*, child,' said the duchess." When I have a problem, sometimes I fret until I find a way to solve it. *Fret* means to worry. The second word is *radiant*. What word? *Radiant* means glowing with happiness. [Indicate the next page.] "Irene in her ordinary dress was *radiant*." A new mother might look radiant when she first holds her baby. *Radiant* means glowing with happiness.

(continued)

Lesson 14
Book Talk and Tier Two Vocabulary Review

Book Talk
Now we have finished reading four books by William Steig. Here they are. Let's take a vote. Who liked *Shrek!* best? Why? [Repeat this process with the other three books.] Remember that three of these books were fantasies because they contain things that can't really happen. If you like fantasies and if you like William Steig's books, you might want to read *Sylvester and the Magic Pebble* (2005). [Hold up book.] This book is about a donkey who wished for the wrong thing. It's a very good story and you'll like the pictures too. See the gold medal on the cover? William Steig won an award for the illustrations in this book. It's right here in our classroom library.

Vocabulary Review
Now we are going to review the words we learned in these books. Here is a list of the words. [Distribute list of Tier 2 words.] As I say each one, put your finger under it. I will remind you of what each word means, and I will also use it in a new sentence. Sometimes I'll ask you questions about the words, so be ready! The first word is *instantly*. Point to it. *Instantly* means right away. When I put sugar in my tea it becomes sweeter instantly. The next word is *specialize*. *Specialize* means to learn just one thing until you are an expert. The doctor specialized in eyes. Do you think you can specialize instantly? Why? The next word is *disgusting*. *Disgusting* means bad mannered or gross. It is disgusting to wipe your dirty hands on your clothes. The next word is *separate*. *Separate* means to put things into different places. I separate my clothes into piles before I wash them. Would you like to separate yourself from a disgusting person? The next word is *wander*. To *wander* means to travel without any place to go. He wandered from place to place looking for adventure. The next word is *shriek*. *Shriek* means to cry out loudly. "Get the spider away from me!" the lady shrieked. The next word is *hideous*. *Hideous* means very ugly. The monster was so hideous we couldn't even look at it. Do you think a person would shriek at something hideous? The next word is *appalled*. *Appalled* means shocked or surprised at something very bad. I was appalled at the bad words I heard in the movie. The next word is *regular*. *Regular* means usual or what happens most of the time. Sometimes you might not get to school at the regular time. Do you think you might be appalled by something if it happened regularly? The next word is *assistant*. An *assistant* is a helper. The magician's assistant helped him do the magic trick. The next word is *announce*. *Announce* means to tell people something important. The man and woman announced that they were getting married. Could an assistant principal make an announcement on the intercom? The next word is *misery*. *Misery* means feeling great pain. My headache caused me a lot of misery. The next word is *promptly*. *Promptly* means right on time. Turn your work in promptly please. If a woman is in real misery, would she like to get help promptly?

(continued)

The next word is *lug*. Lug means to carry something heavy. She lugged her suitcase all the way home.

The next word is *mend*. Mend means to fix something by sewing it. The man mended his shirt with a needle and thread.

Could you lug something and then mend it? What might it be?

The next word is *immense*. Immense means very big or very much. He gave an immense yawn and then fell asleep.

The next word is *dreadful*. Dreadful refers to something you do not like. The noise of the honking cars was dreadful.

Tell me something that is immense and dreadful at the same time.

The next word is *attend*. Attend means to come to a place where others are meeting. I'm sorry but I will be unable to attend your party.

The next word is *desperate*. Desperate means needing help right away. The man was desperate to have his car fixed.

Can you imagine someone being desperate to attend a party?

The next word is *pity*. Pity means feeling sorry for someone. I pity those poor people whose home burned down.

The next word is *manage*. Manage means to do something very hard. The team managed to win at the very last moment.

Could you ever manage to feel pity for someone rich, like the duchess?

The next word is *splendid*. Splendid means wonderful. It was a splendid day and the sun shone brightly.

The next word is *plod*. Plod means to walk when you are very tired. After traveling all day long, the horse plodded toward home.

If you were plodding along, would the end of your journey seem splendid?

The next word is *clutch*. Clutch means to hold something tightly. The child clutched his mother's hand as they crossed the street.

The next word is *fret*. Fret means to worry. Don't fret about silly things; save your fretting for the important ones.

Think of something you might clutch because you were fretting about losing it.

The last word is *radiant*. Radiant means glowing with happiness. After winning the race, the girl wore a radiant smile.

Think of something that might give you a radiant smile.

Now I want you to choose one of these words and write it in a sentence that will show me you know what it means.

instantly	assistant	desperate
specialize	announce	pity
disgusting	misery	manage
separate	promptly	splendid
wander	lug	plod
shriek	mend	clutch
hideous	immense	fret
appalled	dreadful	radiant
regular	attend	

Chapter 7

MAKING DIFFERENTIATION SCHOOLWIDE

In *Differentiated Reading Instruction: Strategies for the Primary Grades* (Walpole & McKenna, 2007), we formulated a model of differentiated instruction that we thought to be consistent with research and reasonable for implementation. Since that time, we have worked with state leaders, district officials, principals, and teachers to understand how best to make that model accessible. What we learned is that many teachers embraced the model conceptually but struggled to plan instruction entirely consistent with it. They understood the "why" of our model, but they had very specific questions about the "how." Other teachers were skeptical about whether the model was viable in terms of planning and implementation. In this volume, we have tried to address the concerns of both sets of teachers—we have tried to show teachers how and at the same time provide them with fully planned lesson cycles. Our sample lessons illustrate our thinking about development and instruction. But they do not constitute a full curriculum. Rather, they provide a series of scaffolds so that teachers can experience cycles of differentiated reading instruction before engaging in their own planning. We will have been successful, though, only when teachers can plan and evaluate their own differentiated lessons.

While we are steadfast in our advocacy for differentiated instruction, we also recognize that it is asking more of an already-stretched-thin workforce. Who does the asking and how that request is supported are critical factors in the success of differentiated instruction. While we are confident that a single classroom teacher can choose to implement differentiated reading instruction, we are also hopeful that schools and districts will engage grade-level teams in systematic differentiation efforts in order to implement high-quality RTI plans. Such collaborative commitment must be nurtured at the building and district levels. In this chapter, we share our reflections on policies and practices that we have seen influence teachers' collective commitment to differentiated instruction.

FACTORS INFLUENCING MOTIVATION

We assume, from the start, that teacher motivation is important to differentiation; we assume that building internal motivation is more effective than building external motivation. Teachers must be motivated to identify their children's needs, to gather additional instructional materials, to plan meaningful reading and writing practice—each of these actions takes time. We assume that internal motivation is influenced by knowledge; teachers are motivated to act based on a complex interplay among three types of knowledge. Their motivation is influenced by their knowledge of reading and language development, their knowledge of their own children's developmental status, and their knowledge of pedagogy. We also assume that internal motivation is influenced by characteristics of the school climate in which teachers work. In particular, teachers' motivation to try new things is influenced by the school's level of acceptance of innovations—including the school's tolerance for missteps and failures. And finally, we assume that teacher motivation for differentiation is affected by their access to the tools they need. In schools where teachers share access to a rich set of books and materials, motivation to try new things is increased.

In Chapter 2 we advocated for assessment strategies consistent with differentiation, and in subsequent chapters we described assessments necessary to identify children for a type of differentiated lesson and assessments necessary to evaluate the effectiveness of a series of lessons. With schools awash in data, calling for more testing is not a comfortable position to take. But data are more than categories and numbers. Data are facts used in analysis. Therefore, teachers' beliefs about the validity of the facts determine the extent to which they are willing to use those facts to make decisions. Differentiation demands usable, understandable data.

For teachers to commit to our version of differentiated reading instruction, they have to commit to instructional improvement. Instructional improvement is not simple. Instructional improvement requires teachers to admit that they are not satisfied with the status quo. Instructional improvement demands a belief that things can become better, and that additional efforts, even those requiring more time and energy, are worthwhile. Instructional improvement demands a commitment to conscious reflection and continuous inquiry. For differentiated instruction to infuse an entire school's curriculum, systems thinking is necessary. Our system, represented in Figure 7.1, comprises usable data,

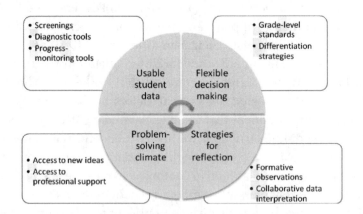

FIGURE 7.1. A system to support differentiated reading instruction.

flexible decision making, strategies for reflection, and a problem-solving climate. The system links teachers to one another and informs the work of teacher leaders—coaches, principals, and district instructional staff.

USABLE STUDENT ACHIEVEMENT DATA

Although we have already devoted an entire chapter to assessment, it is essential to return to those ideas now as we consider schoolwide change. Our experience tells us that it is the *specificity* and *utility* of the data system in a particular school that really determines the school's ability to understand achievement and to target instruction. In fact, it seems that schools are likely to have too much data to process rather than too little. The collection (and often the reporting to parents and school boards) of useless data wastes valuable instructional time, saps teachers' instructional will, and clouds teachers' understanding of achievement. For example, many school systems have simply added new assessments on top of old ones; they have developed district-specific benchmarking assessments, with no attention to validity and reliability, to guide the assignment of grades on report cards and have then required teachers to implement different assessment systems to guide grouping and instruction. Those two sets of assessments rarely yield the same results for children. These competing results put teachers in an uncomfortable position and may make them skeptical about using data to make instructional decisions.

Implications for Teachers

For teachers, a usable data set answers questions that are directly relevant to their work. Screenings (in multiple areas) answer these questions: Which students appear to be struggling? Which of them need additional assessments? Diagnostic assessments answer these questions: What is this student struggling with? What specific skills do I need to teach him or her? Progress monitoring assessments answer these questions: Was my instruction effective for those students? What should I do next? And, finally, outcome assessments answer two very general questions: Is the entire instructional program provided by me and by my colleagues consistent with district, state, and national goals? Is it serving students similarly, regardless of their race, ethnicity, or gender?

Teachers fall into routine data collection that is not connected to any real instructional system. For example, they may assign and test lists of spelling words or high-frequency words that are not part of their instructional program. They may use weekly basal assessments that take time to implement and time to grade, but are never used to guide reteaching or acceleration of the curriculum. They may use inventories to track student development over time without actually intervening by changing their instruction. This type of data collection clouds our focus on differentiation.

Teachers who have a usable data set can take individual student data and identify individual student needs. They can then use that data to group students with similar needs and plan for instruction. Following instruction, they can decide whether to continue in a similar vein or to change their focus. If they analyze data within a grade-level team, they can learn from the successes and failures of their peers. Such usable data forms the basis for assignment into our differentiated lessons and for evaluation of their effectiveness. Such usable data will be essential if teachers are to plan differentiated reading instruction on their own.

Implications for Teacher Leaders

Since we view schools as collaborative instructional environments, with teacher leaders supporting the work of teachers, those leaders have a responsibility to gather and interpret data. Teachers are not often in a position to change district or building requirements for data collection. Teacher leaders are. Teacher leaders must be careful stewards of resources, saving the time and money that is wasted by layering new assessments over old ones. Teacher leaders must ensure that reports to parents reflect the data used to plan instruction and that those data are predictive of later high-stakes decisions. Teacher leaders who want differentiation to take hold in their buildings must be proactive in the creation of a usable data set.

Teacher leaders have responsibilities once that data set is available. Teacher leaders can serve as critical friends while teachers decide how to group students for instruction. Teacher leaders can ensure that instructional plans are consistent with instructional needs. Teacher leaders can capitalize on effective differentiation practices by tracking data and identifying groups with high levels of success. Such success should be celebrated and imitated.

Teacher leaders also have the responsibility for responsible interpretation of outcome data. Outcome data (like screening data) lend themselves only to general interpretations about program effectiveness. If teacher leaders use outcome data as if they were diagnostic, they will circumvent the diagnostic thinking that is the foundation of our differentiation plan. State testing never answers the key differentiation question: What should I teach this child tomorrow?

Mistakes to Avoid

Teachers and teacher leaders can work together to avoid some mistakes that we see as common:

- Using screening data as if they were diagnostic data.
- Using outcome data as if they were diagnostic data.
- Neglecting to collect data to answer the most important teacher-level question: To what extent did the children learn what I was teaching?
- Making high-stakes decisions from data that are neither reliable nor valid.
- Collecting data that are never used in any analysis.

A systems approach to differentiated instruction has, at its foundation, a high-utility data set.

FLEXIBLE DECISION MAKING

While we know that individual teachers can make a tremendous difference in the lives of children, our target has always been grade-level teams working together in schools. We have championed both choice and consistency. We support state and district rights to make their own choices about curriculum and assessment. One of the strange lessons we have learned from our work in schools, however, is that few individuals have an up-to-date notion of what those choices actually are. In many instances, we get different answers to important questions, even from teachers at the same grade level in the same school. How much time is set aside for grade-level instruction? How are students selected for intensive interventions? How are instructional support staff assigned to support teachers and children? What commercial materials are teachers required to use? In what areas are teachers allowed to plan individually? In what areas are they required to plan collaboratively? If we chase those answers back to their source (e.g., the district leader) often we get an answer that references federal or state law, a reference that might be wrong or out of date.

We do not fault the staff who are unclear about guidelines. Designing curriculum is complicated and takes a tremendous amount of time and effort. Unfortunately, a district sometimes figures out how to implement a particular initiative just as a new one is introduced. We simply have to accept that fact and continue to work to understand both the standardized requirements of a particular school and also the specific freedoms (and responsibilities) that teachers have. This section may be counterintuitive, but in order to make flexible differentiation decisions, teachers must think carefully about how and when they will provide grade-level instruction.

Implications for Teachers

Teachers do not seem to embrace curriculum-mapping exercises, but we think that they are essential to differentiation. In our system, we rely on the fact that there is a clear, rigorous, grade-level curriculum in place. That curriculum provides the benchmarks that are necessary for differentiation decisions. We do not want teachers to differentiate for concepts that have not yet been taught; in fact, as we outlined in Chapter 6, if children have learned everything that has been taught in grade-level instruction, we want teachers to build their concept knowledge and vocabulary and to extend their application of comprehension strategies to more challenging texts. In order to make this decision, though, teachers have to understand the order in which skills and strategies will be taught across the year and the order in which they were taught in the previous year. Thus, flexible decision making about differentiation requires consistent fidelity, within and across grade levels, to the scope and sequence underlying the core instructional program.

Implications for Teacher Leaders

An individual teacher can take responsibility for understanding his or her curriculum, but not for ensuring that children received similar grade-level instruction in the previous year. Such a commitment must be fostered (and perhaps required) by teacher leaders. Teacher leaders must take responsibility for communicating clear expectations to the instructional staff and for providing support for high-quality, consistent implementation of those expectations. In addition, teacher leaders must be clear about areas in which teachers are free to make individual decisions, and they must support those decisions when they are of high quality. Each year, then, when children are promoted from one grade level to the next within the same school, the next teacher can begin to plan differentiated reading instruction assuming that all of the children had an initial opportunity to learn grade-level materials, regardless of their homeroom assignment.

Teacher leaders must make curriculum mandates work together. We have worked with districts that give their teachers commercial basal readers (informed by a specific scope and sequence) *and* state standards and curriculum manuals (informed by a different scope and sequence) *and* district curriculum manuals (informed by yet a third scope and sequence). Often, as represented in Figure 7.2, the differences in these guidelines are much wider than the consistencies.

Schoolwide implementation of differentiated reading instruction is impossible in such a curriculum climate; the complexity and inconsistency of the guidance guarantees that teachers will make sense of their professional responsibilities in inconsistent ways. An alternative to such a plan is a system in which teacher leaders are clear with teachers about exactly how and why particular grade-level curriculum materials and instructional strategies, used specifically and consistently, enable teams to meet state and district requirements.

Finally, teacher leaders have a responsibility to make federally funded programs (e.g., special education, Title I) work together in a particular school. That means that services provided by those programs, assessments within those programs, scheduling of those programs, and professional support associated with those programs must evolve continuously as the school's instructional program evolves. Teacher leaders (rather than teachers themselves) must ask the questions: How can we make sure that this improvement is realized in all of our programs? How will this change affect resources in other programs? How can we make our support of student achievement seamless?

Mistakes to Avoid

Remember our goal is to motivate all teachers in a school to do the work required for differentiated reading instruction. A system that accomplishes this goal will balance accountability with freedom and high expectations for instruction. The mistakes listed below sap teachers' collective and individual commitment to differentiation:

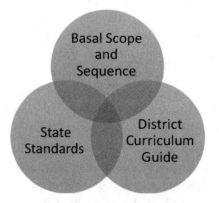

FIGURE 7.2. Potentially conflicting guidance for teachers.

- Failing to provide (or use) time for grade-level, team-based decision making.
- Allowing each teacher total freedom.
- Allowing each teacher no freedom.
- Adding new programs, requirements, or procedures on top of old ones rather than revising the total plan.

Although teacher leaders have extensive responsibilities in this area, they can meet those responsibilities with extensive teacher involvement and input. That effort can fuel the reflection that we describe next.

STRATEGIES FOR REFLECTION

When teachers and teacher leaders commit to a system of usable data and engage in flexible, team-based decision making about grade-level instruction and differentiated instruction, it makes sense to reflect on whether those decisions are yielding results. Often, that reflection is summative. Schools make commitments at the beginning of the year, and then they wait for the end-of-year data to see whether those commitments were justified. What is missing from such thinking is analysis of whether and how well those commitments were actually realized. Teachers and teacher leaders have to work together to observe the curriculum in action before making any decisions about its effectiveness.

Implications for Teachers

Teachers who engage in reflection about the effectiveness of their instruction need access to three types of data. They need to know how frequently they implemented it. They need to know how well they implemented it. And they need to know whether students benefited from it. Some of that work can be done within the classroom. Teachers can work with teammates to draft reasonable instructional schedules, and they can keep track, in their own classrooms, of how well they can keep to those schedules. In the case of differentiated reading instruction, teachers can begin by using our plans and marking the time and date when they used each portion of each plan. That kind of personal reflection answers an important question: How often and for how long did I try to do it? But it leaves another question unanswered: How well did I do it? Only an observer can begin to answer this important question.

If teachers are to engage in real reflection, they have to be open to collecting data on "how well." That means that they must be open to ongoing formative observation. They must begin by opening their doors to principals and coaches and peers who can give confidential feedback about the quality of instruction; they must be willing to accept that not all observation is evaluative and not all observation is negative. They also must be willing to accept feedback that includes specific areas for improvement. That type of feedback is essential to improving instructional quality before making decisions about instructional effectiveness.

Implications for Teacher Leaders

Teacher leaders have extensive responsibilities in setting the climate for reflection. If their goal is to determine the extent to which the curriculum choices they have made—including their commitment to differentiated reading instruction—are getting the results they want, they have to gauge the extent to which all teachers are trying to implement those choices and they have to provide professional support to those who need it. In effect, teacher leaders must be able to deliver differentiated professional support for teachers who are trying to provide differentiated instruction for children.

Formative observation is at the heart of real reflection. Formative observation requires a true commitment to confidentiality and a clear separation of observations for the purpose of planning professional support from observations for the purpose of personnel evaluation. Formative observations require time; they require ongoing brief walk-throughs of all classrooms (where teacher leaders can reflect on how well teachers can implement the instructional schedule, among other things), longer targeted observations of specific parts of the instructional program (where teacher leaders can reflect on how well a particular teacher can implement that portion of the instructional plan and then provide feedback and support for improvements), and even longer full observations (where teacher leaders can reflect on how well a particular teacher can juggle the demands of grade-level instruction and differentiate instruction). In the most intensive (and expensive) implementations, both a principal and a literacy coach engage in formative observation on a daily basis.

Teacher leaders who want to engage teachers in reflection must be specific about what they are looking for and specific in their feedback. Checklists and rubrics can guide formative observation and reassure teachers who are unaccustomed to reflection. Such observation tools can be constructed with teacher input to reflect the instructional commitments that they have made, and then used to target feedback and plan differentiated professional support.

Mistakes to Avoid

We have extensive experience in formative observation as the foundation for reflection about instructional choices. We have made many of the mistakes below, and we urge you to plan to avoid them:

- Lack of grade-level or team-based instructional commitments.
- Failure to take advantage of brief walk-throughs.
- Lack of procedures for formative observation.
- Delay in providing feedback to teachers.
- Failure to provide teachers with support for improvements once they have been identified.

If you can implement a formative assessment system, you will know whether you need to improve teachers' ability to implement the choices that you have made together or whether you need to make new instructional choices, a possibility we explore next.

PROBLEM-SOLVING CLIMATE

One of the most troublesome aspects of implementing our model of differentiated reading instruction is that sometimes teachers will be wrong. In fact, the model assumes it. If, after 3 weeks of instruction, delivered well, some students have not learned what a teacher has tried to teach, he or she will know it, and will have to try to figure out why. One possible explanation is that the instruction the teacher planned and implemented was too challenging—the data used did not reveal the actual instructional needs for that student. Another possibility is that the instructional strategies the teacher used were not intensive enough to address the student's needs. Being wrong is a problem, and it is not comfortable. However, it is possible for teachers and teacher leaders to work together to assume that problems are a natural part of teaching and to solve those problems together.

Implications for Teachers

In order for teachers to engage in problem solving, their most important responsibility is to be honest about their problems. Our model of differentiated reading instruction asks teachers to use data to identify needs and form groups, to plan for 3 weeks of targeted instruction, and then to evaluate the effectiveness of that instruction, potentially regrouping students and definitely planning new lessons. If teachers engage in that evaluation and planning in groups, they can identify problems collaboratively and share possible solutions. They can reflect together about what worked for a particular student or type of student. They can also share failures, helping colleagues to avoid mistakes by sharing what did not work. That kind of problem-solving atmosphere requires an initial leap of faith, but helps to shape a much more comfortable, less isolated work environment.

Implications for Teacher Leaders

Teacher leaders have responsibilities here too. First, they must constantly model problem-solving behaviors, admitting their own mistakes, accepting collegial feedback, and committing to try new approaches. They must support teachers and acknowledge their efforts to change what they are doing in order to serve students better.

Collegiality takes time, and teacher leaders can provide teachers with time to solve problems together. They can schedule the instructional day so that grade-level teams have common planning periods. They can hire substitute teachers to provide half-day planning sessions for teams. They can use faculty meeting time for collegial work rather than business that could be conducted electronically. They can make good use of building-level professional development days.

But not all problems can be solved by the staff, even if they have time to collaborate. Sometimes the problems require solutions that no one knows about. Not all solutions that teachers might suggest are equally likely to yield improved achievement. Not all solutions are consistent with the curriculum choices that the school has already made. We read to keep abreast of the scientific literature in the areas of reading development, reading assessment, and reading instruction. We read books and articles, and we recommend books and articles for team-based study. Teacher leaders have to ensure that problem-solving efforts are informed by the best available evidence. They have to stay current, and they have to help their teachers to stay current. They have to ensure that teachers have access to a fully functional professional support system, constantly infused with new ideas.

Mistakes to Avoid

Establishing a problem-solving climate is not a simple task, but it is well worth the effort. Differentiated reading instruction at the school level requires it, but we think that it will yield benefits in other areas of the curriculum. Here are some mistakes to avoid and problems to address:

- Teacher fear to admit that students are not learning.
- Lack of attention to finding new ideas.
- Uncritically honoring all input from teachers and teacher leaders.
- Commitment to ideas, programs, and strategies *even when they do not work.*
- Settling for compromises between what works and what doesn't.
- Bandwagon-based commitments to new programs before their efficacy has been established.
- Program evaluation without reflection on the quality of instruction.

One thing is certain. If teachers are really committed to differentiation, sometimes their decisions will be wrong. They will not be wrong for long, though. Every 3 weeks, they will have a chance to evaluate them. And, if a school is making the commitment to try our model, teachers will have colleagues to help them.

A FINAL PLEA

We know that teachers work hard. We know that the demands they face are increasingly complex. We know that planning differentiated reading instruction is yet another demand. Here are a few points to consider before you jump in with both feet.

You can start to differentiate with just one group at a time. Think about students you are most worried about, and start there. It might be the low-achieving children in your class, but it also might be the high-achieving children. Start there, and see whether you can use a set of our lessons. Be critical, evaluating whether these procedures provide challenge and new learning opportunities. If they do, consider adding another group.

When you have exhausted our lessons, plan your own. Take advantage of what you learned works in our lessons and repeat it. Do not repeat what does not work for your students. Save your plans, and share them with your colleagues. The burden of planning can be considerably reduced by adopting a team approach. The learning curve for planning differentiated reading instruction is steep. Your first set of plans will take a lot of time, but then you will get the hang of it. We did.

REFERENCES

Adams, M. J. (1990). *Beginning to read: Thinking and learning about print*. Cambridge, MA: MIT Press.

Adler, D. (1993). *Cam Jansen and the chocolate fudge mystery*. New York: Puffin Books.

Ash, G. E., & Kuhn, M. R. (2006). Meaningful oral and silent reading in the elementary and middle school classroom. In T. Rasinski, C. Blachowicz, & K. Lems (Eds.), *Fluency instruction: Research-based best practices* (pp. 155–172). New York: Guilford Press.

Ball, E. W., & Blachman, B. A. (1991). Does phoneme awareness training in kindergarten make a difference in early word recognition and developmental spelling? *Reading Research Quarterly, 26*, 49–66.

Barr, R. (1992). Teachers, materials, and group composition in literacy instruction. In M. J. Dreher & W. H. Slater (Eds.), *Elementary school literacy: Critical issues* (pp. 27–50). Norwood, MA: Christopher-Gordon.

Bear, D. R., Invernizzi, M., Templeton, S. R., & Johnston, F. (2008). *Words their way: Word study for phonics, vocabulary, and spelling instruction* (4th ed.). Upper Saddle River, NJ: Prentice Hall.

Beck, I. L., McKeown, M. G., & Kucan, L. (2002). *Bringing words to life: Robust vocabulary instruction*. New York: Guilford Press.

Biemiller, A. (2004). Teaching vocabulary in the primary grades: Vocabulary instruction needed. In J. F. Baumann & E. J. Kame'enui (Eds.), *Vocabulary instruction: Research to practice* (pp. 28–40). New York: Guilford Press.

Block, C. C., & Paris, S. R. (Eds.). (2002). *Comprehension instruction: Research-based best practices* (2nd ed.). New York: Guilford Press.

Brown, M. (1986). *Arthur's teacher trouble*. Boston: Little, Brown.

Carnine, D. W., Silbert, J., Kame'enui, E. J., Tarver, S. G., & Jungjohann, K. (2006). *Teaching struggling and at-risk readers: A direct instruction approach*. Upper Saddle River, NJ: Prentice Hall.

Chall, J. S. (1983/1996). *Stages of reading development*. New York: McGraw-Hill.

Chard, D. J., Pikulski, J. J., & McDonagh, S. H. (2006). Fluency: The link between decoding and comprehension for struggling readers. In T. Rasinski, C. Blachowicz, & K. Lems (Eds.), *Fluency instruction: Research-based best practices* (pp. 39–61). New York: Guilford Press.

Clements, A. (2001). *Jake Drake, bullybuster*. New York: Simon & Schuster.

Duffy, G. G. (2009). *Explaining reading: A resource for teaching concepts, skills, and strategies* (2nd ed.). New York: Guilford Press.

Duke, N. K. (2000). 3.6 minutes per day: The scarcity of informational texts in first grade. *Reading Research Quarterly, 35*, 202–224.

Duke, N. K., & Bennett-Armistead, V. S. (2003). *Reading and writing informational text in the primary grades: Research-based practices.* New York: Scholastic.

Durkin, D. (1978). What classroom observations reveal about reading comprehension instruction. *Reading Research Quarterly, 14*, 481–533.

Ehri, L. (1995). Phases of development in learning to read words by sight. *Journal of Research in Reading, 18*, 116–125.

Ehri, L. (1997). Sight word learning in normal readers and dyslexics. In B. Blachman (Ed.), *Foundations of reading acquisition and dyslexia: Implications for early intervention* (pp. 163–189). Mahwah, NJ: Erlbaum.

Esbensen, B. J. (1994). *Baby whales drink milk.* New York: HarperCollins.

Ezell, H. K., & Justice, L. M. (2000). Increasing the print focus of adult–child shared book reading through observational learning. *American Journal of Speech–Language Pathology, 9*, 36–47.

Fountas, I. C., & Pinnell, G. S. (1996). *Guided reading: Good first teaching for all children.* Portsmouth, NH: Heinemann.

Ganske, K. (2000). *Word journeys: Assessment-guided phonics, spelling, and vocabulary instruction.* New York: Guilford Press.

Gaskins, I. W. (2005). *Success with struggling readers: The Benchmark School approach.* New York: Guilford Press.

Gibbons, G. (1992). *Recycle!: A handbook for kids.* Boston: Little, Brown.

Gibbons, G. (2008). *The planets* (3rd ed.). New York: Holiday House.

Hasbrouck, J., & Tindal, G. A. (2006). Oral reading fluency norms: A valuable assessment tool for reading teachers. *The Reading Teacher, 59*, 636–644.

Hodge, D. (1999). *Whales: Killer whales, blue whales and more.* Toronto: Kids Can Press.

Hoff, S. (1961). *Albert the albatross.* New York: Harper.

Hosp, M. K., Hosp, J. L., & Howell, K. W. (2007). *The ABCs of CBM: A practical guide to curriculum-based measurement.* New York: Guilford Press.

James, S. M. (2002). *Dolphins.* New York: Mondo.

Jenkins, J., Vadasy, P., & Peyton, J. (2003). Decodable text—where to find it. *The Reading Teacher, 57*, 185–189.

Joyce, B., & Showers, B. (2002). *Student achievement through staff development* (3rd ed.). Alexandria, VA: Association for Supervision and Curriculum Development.

Justice, L. M., & Ezell, H. K. (2002). Use of storybook reading to increase print awareness in at-risk children. *American Journal of Speech–Language Pathology, 11*, 17–29.

Kraus, R. (1986). *Whose mouse are you?* New York: Aladdin Books.

Kuhn, M. R., & Stahl, S. A. (2003). Fluency: A review of developmental and remedial practices. *Journal of Educational Psychology, 95*, 3–21.

Kuhn, M. R., & Woo, D. G. (2008). Fluency-oriented reading: Two whole-class approaches. In M. R. Kuhn & P. J. Schwanenflugel (Eds.), *Fluency in the classroom* (pp. 17–35). New York: Guilford Press.

Leslie, L., & Caldwell, J. S. (2005). *Qualitative reading inventory—4.* New York: Allyn & Bacon.

McCully, E. A. (1996). *The ballot box battle.* New York: Knopf.

McKenna, M. C., & Dougherty Stahl, K. A. D. (2009). *Assessment for reading instruction* (2nd ed.). New York: Guilford Press.

McKenna, M. C., & Robinson, R. D. (2009). *Teaching through text: A content literacy approach to content area reading.* Boston: Allyn & Bacon/Vango.

McKenna, M. C., & Walpole, S. (2005). How well does assessment inform our reading instruction? *The Reading Teacher, 59,* 84–86.

Meisinger, E. B., & Bradley, B. A. (2008). Classroom practices for supporting fluency development. In M. R. Kuhn & P. J. Schwanenflugel (Eds.), *Fluency in the classroom* (pp. 36–54). New York: Guilford Press.

Moskal, M. K., & Blachowicz, C. (2006). *Partnering for fluency.* New York: Guilford Press.

National Assessment of Educational Progress. (2007). *The nation's report card.* Washington, DC: U.S. Department of Education. Available at *nationsreportcard.gov/reading_2007.*

Neuman, S. B., Copple, C., & Bredekamp, S. (2000). *Learning to read and write: Developmentally appropriate practices for young children.* Washington, DC: National Association for the Education of Young Children.

Paratore, J. R., & McCormack, R. L. (2005). *Teaching literacy in second grade.* New York: Guilford Press.

Paris, S. G., Searnio, D. A., & Cross, D. R. (1986). A metacognitive curriculum to promote children's reading and learning. *Australian Journal of Psychology, 38*(2), 107–123.

Rasinski, T. V. (2003). *The fluent reader: Oral reading strategies for building word recognition, fluency, and comprehension.* New York: Scholastic.

Rylant, C. (1996). *Henry and Mudge: The first book.* New York: Simon & Schuster.

Rylant, C. (1996). *Henry and Mudge: The green time.* New York: Simon & Schuster.

Rylant, C. (1996). *Henry and Mudge: Puddle trouble.* New York: Simon & Schuster.

Rylant, C. (1996). *Henry and Mudge: Sparkle days.* New York: Simon & Schuster.

Rylant, C. (1996). *Henry and Mudge: Under the yellow moon.* New York: Simon & Schuster.

Rylant, C. (2003). *Henry and Mudge and Mrs. Hopper's house.* New York: Simon & Schuster.

Samuels, S. J. (1979). The method of repeated readings. *The Reading Teacher, 32,* 241–254.

Schell, L. M., & Hanna, G. S. (1981). Can informal reading inventories reveal strengths and weaknesses in comprehension subskills? *The Reading Teacher, 35,* 263–268.

Schwanenflugel, P. J., & Ruston, H. P. (2008). Becoming a fluent reader: From theory to practice. In M. R. Kuhn & P. J. Schwanenflugel (Eds.), *Fluency in the classroom* (pp. 1–16). New York: Guilford Press.

Scieszka, J. (2000). *See you later, gladiator.* New York: Viking.

Shanahan, T. (2006). Developing fluency in the context of effective literacy instruction. In T. Rasinski, C. Blachowicz, & K. Lems (Eds.), *Fluency instruction: Research-based best practices* (pp. 21–38). New York: Guilford Press.

Sharmat, M. W. (2007). *Nate the Great and the missing key.* New York: Yearling.

Simon, S. (2002). *Killer whales.* New York: Sea Star Books.

Smolkin, L. B., & Donovan, C. A. (2002). "Oh, excellent, excellent question!": Developmental differences and comprehension acquisition. In C. C. Block & M. Pressley (Eds.), *Comprehension instruction: Research-based best practices* (pp. 140–157). New York: Guilford Press.

Spector, J. E. (2005). How reliable are informal reading inventories? *Psychology in the Schools, 42,* 593–603.

Stahl, K. A. D. (2008). Creating opportunities for comprehension instruction within fluency-oriented reading. In M. R. Kuhn & P. J. Schwanenflugel (Eds.), *Fluency in the classroom* (pp. 55–74). New York: Guilford Press.

Stahl, K. A. D. (2009). Assessing comprehension of young children. In S. E. Israel & G. G. Duffy (Eds.), *Handbook of research on reading comprehension.* New York: Routledge.

Stahl, S. A., & Heubach, K. M. (2005). Fluency-oriented reading instruction. *Journal of Literacy Research, 37,* 25–60.

Stahl, S. A., Kuhn, M. R., & Pickle, J. M. (1999). An educational model of assessment and targeted instruction for children with reading problems. In D. H. Evensen & P. B. Mosenthal (Eds.), *Advances in reading/language research: Reconsidering the role of the reading clinic in a new age of literacy* (pp. 249–272). Stamford, CT: JAI Press.

Stahl, S. A., & Nagy, W. E. (2005). *Teaching word meanings.* Mahwah, NJ: Erlbaum.

Steig, W. (1977). *Amos and Boris.* New York: Puffin Books.

Steig, W. (1986). *Brave Irene.* New York: Farrar, Strauss, & Giroux.

Steig, W. (1992). *Doctor De Soto.* New York: Farrar, Strauss, & Giroux.

Steig, W. (2001). *Shrek* [Film]. Dream Works Pictures.

Steig, W. (2005). *Sylvester and the magic pebble.* New York: Simon & Schuster.

Wallbrown, F. H., Brown, D. H., & Engin, A. W. (1978). A factor analysis of reading attitudes along with measures of reading achievement and scholastic aptitude. *Psychology in the Schools, 15,* 160–165.

Walpole, S., & McKenna, M. C. (2004). *The literacy coach's handbook: A guide to research-based practice.* New York: Guilford Press.

Walpole, S., & McKenna, M. C. (2007). *Differentiated reading instruction: Strategies for the primary grades.* New York: Guilford Press.

Wylie, R. E., & Durrell, D. D. (1970). Teaching vowels through phonograms. *Elementary English, 47,* 787–791.

Yep, L. (1993). *The man who tricked a ghost.* Mahwah, NJ: Bridgewater Press.

INDEX

Page numbers in *italic* indicate a figure or table

Achievement data
  benefits of specificity and utility in, 161
  implications for teacher leaders, 162
  implications for teachers, 161–162
  mistakes to avoid with, 162
Albert the Albatross (Hoff), *102*
Alphabet, teaching directly, 23–24
Analogy, decoding by, 58
Arthur's Teacher Trouble (Brown), *102*
Assessed needs, differentiation by, 4
Assessments
  assessment cycle for small-group instruction, *11*
  importance of, 11
  of needs, 13–14
  Tier I instruction and, 5
  types of, 11–13
  using to form small groups, 14, *15, 16*
  using to match books and children, 16–18
  using to plan and evaluate instruction, 15–16
Author study cycle for grades 2–3, 147–158

B

Ballot Box Battle, The (McCully), *102*
Basic Alphabet Knowledge group
  assessment, 39, 40
  choices for instruction, 27
  choosing the instructional focus, *23*
  generic lesson plan, 29
  high-frequency-word materials, 37–38
  materials for letter names, 35–36
  materials for sound sorting, 33–34
  planning instruction for, 22, 23–24
  sample script, 30
  words for initial sound sorting, 31–32
"Basic alphabet knowledge" instruction, 20
Benchmark School, 21
Blends, 61, *62*
Blends and Digraphs group
  assessment, 74
  concepts to master, 56
  generic lesson plan, 69
  instructional choices with, 65–66
  planning instruction for, 61, *62*
  sample script, 70
  words for sounding and blending, 71–73
Books
  assessing suitability for fluency instruction, 17
  assessing suitability for read-alouds, 17
  assessing suitability for reading, 18
  for fluency and comprehension group instruction, 100–101
  using assessments to match to children, 16–18
  for vocabulary and comprehension groups, 120–121, *122*
  See also Decodable books
Buddy reading, 106

173

C

Choral reading, 102, 104–105
Cognitive model of reading assessment, 13–14
Comprehension, assessing, 12
Comprehension instruction
  choosing a method for, 124–125, *127–128*
  effective, 13
  planning for, 123–124
Comprehension questions, 107–108
Core reading instruction
  defined, 5
  instructional schedule for, 7–8
Cumulative choral reading, 105
Curriculum-based measurement, 12

D

Decision making
  implications for teacher leaders, 163–164
  implications for teachers, 163
  mistakes to avoid, 164–165
  significance of, 162–163
Decodable books
  assembling for reading practice, 58–59
  commercial sources for, *59*
  template for organizing, *60*
"Developmental shift," 120
Diagnostic assessments, 12
DIBELS battery, 12, 108–109
Differentiated Reading Instruction (Walpole & McKenna), 124, 159
Differentiation
  by assessed needs, 4
  factors influencing motivation in, 160–161
  flexible decision making and, 162–165
  by fluency level, 3
  by instructional level, 2–3
  instructional schedules, 7–8
  instructional tiers, 4–6
  problem-solving climate and, 167–168
  strategies for reflection and, 165–166
  usable student achievement data and, 161–162
Differentiation groups, number of, 8
Digraphs, 61, *62*
Direct instruction, in phonological awareness and word recognition, 21–22
Dynamic Indicators of Basic Early Literacy Skills (DIBELS), 12, 108–109

E

Echo reading, 102, 103–104
End-of-cycle assessments, 15–16
Euclid, 123
Every pupil response
  fluency and comprehension group instruction, 108
  phonological awareness and word recognition instruction, 26
  vocabulary and comprehension instruction, 129–131
  word recognition and fluency instruction, 64, *66*
Expository books, 120–121

F

Federally funded programs, 164
Feedback, 165
Fiction books, teaching vocabulary and, 123
Fluency and Comprehension instruction
  assessing suitability of books for, 17
  assessment, 108–109
  basic lesson structure, *98*
  checklist for targeting, *99*
  choosing books for, 100–101
  choosing instructional methods, 101–103
  choral reading, 104–105
  echo reading, 103–104
  every pupil response, 108
  identifying students who will benefit from, 96–97
  inferential questions, 107–108
  multisyllable decoding practice, 112–114
  overview of, 97–99
  partner reading, 105–106, *107*
  planning for, 99–100, *110*
  sample lessons for a first-grade group, 115
  sample lessons for a second-grade group, 116
  sample lessons for a third-grade group, 117
  syllable types, 103
  whisper reading, 106–107
Fluency instruction
  assessing the suitability of books for, 17
  effective, 12

Fluency level
  assessments, 12
  differentiation by, 3
Fluency-oriented reading instruction, 98–99
Formative observation, 166

G

Grade-level instruction, instructional schedule
  for, 7–8
Group placement, using assessments to make,
  14, *15*, *16*
Guided reading, 3

H

Henry and Mudge and Mrs. Hopper's House
  (Rylant), *102*

I

Inferential questions, 107–108
Informal reading inventories, 2–3
Informational books, 120–121
Instructional reading level, differentiation by,
  2–3
Instructional schedules, 7–8
Instructional tiers, 4–6
Internal motivation, 160

J

Jake Drake, Bully Buster (Clements), *102*

L

Letter Sounds group
  materials for using letter sounds, 46
  words for say-it-and-move-it and sounding
    and blending, 43–45
Lexile Framework, 100–101, *102*
Libraries, of shared texts, 58–59
Listening level, of books, 17
Literacy coaches, 5–6
Little Red Riding Hood, 108

Long-Vowel Teams group
  assessment, 95
  generic lesson plan, 87
  materials for decoding by analogy, 94
  sample script, 88
  words for decoding by analogy, 89–93
  See also Vowel Teams group

M

Man Who Tricked a Ghost, The (Yep), *102*
Motivation, factors influencing, 160–161
Multisyllablic decoding, 101, 103, 112–114

N

Narrative books, 120–121
Nate the Great and the Missing Key (Sharmat),
  102
National Assessment of Educational Progress
  (NAEP), 119
Needs assessment, systematic, 13–14
Nonfiction books
  teaching vocabulary and, 123
  in vocabulary and comprehension instruction,
    120–121

O

Ockham's razor, 1

P

Paired reading, 106
Partner reading, 102–103, 105–106, *107*
Phonological awareness and Word
  recognition
  direct instruction in, 21–22
  entry skills level, 19
  every pupil response, 26
  identifying children who need instruction in,
    19–21
  planning for instruction in, 22–25
Phonological Literacy Screening (PALS), 12
Planets, The (Gibbons), 100
Problem-solving climate, 167–168

Q

Questions, inferential, 107–108

R

R-Controlled Vowels group
assessment, 79
concepts to master, 56–57
generic lesson plan, 75
instructional choices with, 66
planning instruction for, 61–62, *63*
words for sounding and blending, 76–78
Read-aloud cycle, 134–146
Read-alouds, assessing the suitability of books
for, 17
Reading assessment, cognitive model of, 13–14
Reading practice
assembling decodable texts for, 58–59
defined as a term, 7
Recycle! (Gibbons), 128
Reflection, strategies for, 165–166
Response-to-intervention (RTI) model, 5

S

Scholastic Reading Counts, 100, 122
Screening assessment, 11–12
See You Later, Gladiator (Scieszka), *102*
Sight vocabulary, 58
Small-group instruction
assessment cycle for, *11*
by fluency level, 3
should be challenging, 8–9
Small groups
characteristics of children in, *16*
using assessments to form, 14, *15, 16*
Syllable types, 103
Systematic assessment, of needs, 13–14

T

Teacher leaders
flexible decision making about differentiation,
163–164
problem-solving climate and, 167–168
strategies for reflection, 166
usable achievement data and, 162

Teachers
commitment to instructional improvement,
160
flexible decision making about differentiation,
163
problem-solving climate and, 167
strategies for reflection, 165
usable achievement data and, 161–162
Teacher supports, Tier I instruction and, 5–6
Texas Education Agency, 4
Texts. *See* Books; Decodable books
Text structures, 125, 128–129
Tier 2 words, 123
Tiered instruction
instructional schedules, 7–8
overview, 4–6
Tier I, 5–6
Tier II, 6
Tier III, 6

U

Unit assessments, 12
Using Letter Patterns group
assessment, 54
choices for instruction, *23,* 27
generic lesson plan, 48
planning instruction for, 22, 23, 25
sample script, 49
student materials, 51–53
words for, 50
"Using Letter Patterns" instruction, 20–21
Using Letter Sounds group, 22
assessment, 47
choices for instruction, *23,* 27
generic lesson plan, 41
planning instruction for, 24–25
sample script, 42
"Using Letter Sounds" instruction, 20

V

Vocabulary, assessing, 12
Vocabulary and Comprehension instruction
assessing, 131–132
assessing suitability of books for, 17
author study cycle for grades 2–3, 147–158
choosing a method for, 124–129
choosing books for, 120–121, *122*